The Gadamer Dictionary

Also available from Continuum:

The Derrida Dictionary, Simon Morgan Wortham
The Sartre Dictionary, Gary Cox
The Hegel Dictionary, Glenn Magee

Forthcoming:

The Deleuze and Guattari Dictionary, Greg Lambert, Gary Genosko,
    Janell Watson and Eugene B. Young
The Heidegger Dictionary, Daniel O Dahlstrom
The Husserl Dictionary, Dermot Moran and Joseph Cohen
The Kant Dictionary, Lucas Thorpe
The Marx Dictionary, Ian Fraser and Laurence Wilde
The Nietzsche Dictionary, Greg Moore
The Wittgenstein Dictionary, David Levy

The Gadamer Dictionary

Chris Lawn and Niall Keane

continuum

Continuum International Publishing Group
The Tower Building, 11 York Road, London SE1 7NX
80 Maiden Lane, Suite 704, New York NY 10038
www.continuumbooks.com

British Library Cataloguing-in-Publication Data
A catalogue record for this book is available from the British Library.

ISBN: HB: 978-1-8470-6158-4
        PB: 978-1-8470-6159-1

Library of Congress Cataloguing-in-Publication Data
Lawn, Chris.
   The Gadamer dictionary / Chris Lawn and Niall Keane.
      p. cm.
   Includes bibliographical references.
   ISBN 978-1-84706-158-4 -- ISBN 978-1-84706-159-1   1.   Gadamer, Hans-Georg,
1900-2002--Dictionaries.   I. Keane, Niall. II. Title.
   B3248.G34L395 2011
   193--dc22
                          2010038467

Typeset by Fakenham Prepress Solutions Ltd
Printed and bound in India

Contents

Acknowledgements

Although he does not know this, the authors owe a large debt of gratitude to Gary Cox and his *The Sartre Dictionary*. This was the first work in the Continuum series of philosophical dictionaries and we have shamelessly used his pioneering work as a model and continuous reference point for our own.

We also thank the many authors mentioned in our bibliography for the light they have shone on the darker passages in Gadamer's work. Particular thanks must go to Jean Grondin whose biography of his friend and teacher, Gadamer, is one of the best sources of information on his life. We have frequently resorted to Grondin's *Hans-Georg Gadamer: A Biography*.

We would like to take this opportunity to thank Steven Leddin of the Philosophy Department, Mary Immaculate College, University of Limerick, for his careful editing, his contribution to the entries on Adorno and Dialectic, and assistance with the production of the final manuscript. We would also like to thank the Library staff of Mary Immaculate College for their efficiency in supplying inter-library loans and other material.

Some of the entries in the *Dictionary* have been taken from Chris Lawn's *Gadamer: A Guide for the Perplexed*, (New York and London: Continuum, 2006).

Introduction

The work of Hans-Georg Gadamer – unlike a good deal of modern philosophy – is significantly lacking in abstruse and highly technical terminology. Because his work emphasises our dependence upon everyday, that is non-philosophical, language, he is at pains to develop ideas that avoid the all too easy descent into complex and bewildering terminology. This said, Gadamer has spawned a variety of terms and idioms. For example, he speaks of a 'fusion of horizons' and 'effective historical consciousness'. This dictionary is designed to explain in detail these and other such terms at the heart of Gadamer's philosophical project. Gadamer also uses familiar terms, such as 'hermeneutics', 'tradition' and 'dialogue', but they take on specific meanings within his writings and they require a detailed gloss and clarification.

As well as an explanation of specific terms, the dictionary relates these to broader themes. Gadamer works within the distinctly European philosophical traditions of hermeneutics and phenomenology and these have given rise to, and draw upon, their own collection of concepts and ideas not immediately familiar to general readers or those working in the general terrain of analytic or English-language philosophy. This dictionary provides a detailed guide to the key ideas from which Gadamer's own philosophical hermeneutics is drawn. Such a guide will be particularly useful to those unfamiliar with the contours of recent continental philosophy.

Gadamer lived to the venerable old age of 102. He was born in 1900 and died in 2002; if he had been born a year earlier (and died a year earlier) he would have had the rare distinction of having lived through three centuries! Gadamer's longevity is worthy of note not simply for its rarity value but because it says something about the character of his thought. In some ways he is quite an old-fashioned thinker, being educated within the distant cultural milieus of First World War and Weimar Germany. On the other hand, there is something distinctly modern about someone who participates in near-contemporary debates about post-modernity, alterity, relativism and anti-foundationalism. Curiously, Gadamer's international career took off when most people would be thinking of retirement. His magnum opus, *Truth and Method*, was published when he was 60. The book very quickly established itself as a modern classic and Gadamer henceforth embarked upon a new vocation as internationally recognized philosopher. For the next 40 years or so he developed and published his ideas and continued to attend conferences all over the world. *Truth and Method*, the six hundred-page defence of hermeneutics and the human sciences, with its detailed readings of the key texts in the history of philosophy, is at the heart of Gadamer's work. It represents a wealth of scholarship and springs from an engagement with some of the most celebrated thinkers in nineteenth and twentieth century German philosophy.

At the heart of Gadamer's work is a justification of philosophy itself in an intellectual world all too often dominated by the practices and procedures of natural science. For Gadamer, the time-honoured practice of hermeneutics, all but forgotten about in the modern age until revived in the nineteenth century, demonstrates that human understanding cannot be encapsulated in a body of rules or methodology; it operates in all aspects of our attempts to make sense of the world. For this reason, art and the artistry of language tell us as much about the world and ourselves as does the more revered natural science. Gadamer's greatest achievement is to use hermeneutics to re-instate the human sciences.

The Dictionary will enable the reader to explore and understand the key terms in Gadamer's lexicon. It will also enable the reader to grasp the many ideas Gadamer advances on the nature of language, art, history and human understanding. The authors operated according to a fairly strict division of labour. One of us focused on the key terms and concepts in Gadamer's work. The other dealt mainly with broader themes and the entries upon specific historical figures who either influenced Gadamer directly, such as his teachers Husserl and Heidegger, or whose influence was less direct but important, figures such as Hegel or Augustine.

The Dictionary will act as an important point of reference and assist those coming to grips with Gadamer and the whole domain of philosophical hermeneutics. It will also be a valuable aid to those who need information about the many sources on which Gadamer's work draws.

Chronology: Gadamer's Life and Works*

1900   Hans-Georg Gadamer was born in Marburg, Germany, to Johannes Gadamer and Emma Caroline Johanna Gewiese.

1902   The family moves to Breslau in Lower Silesia; in 1945 the once-German city became part of Poland, adopting the Polish name Wrocław.

1904   His mother dies of diabetes.

1905   Gadamer's father remarries.

1918   He attends the University of Breslau and matriculates in German Studies.

1919   The family moves back to Marburg as Johannes Gadamer is made professor at the University.

1919   Gadamer commences studies in philosophy at the University of Marburg.

1922   He contracts polio and spends months in isolation. During this time he reads Husserl and some unpublished work of Heidegger. He starts to fall under the influence of Heidegger and resolves to study with him in Freiburg.

1923   Gadamer marries Frida Kratz, daughter of a factory owner and a friend from Breslau, who nursed him through his illness with polio.

1923   He attends Heidegger's classes in Freiburg.

1925   Gadamer starts intensive study of classical philology after Heidegger rebukes him and causes him to doubt his abilities in philosophy.

1926   Jutta, Gadamer's first daughter, is born.

1927   He passes the examination in classical philology and is awarded the
        Habilitation.

1928   Johannes Gadamer dies of cancer.

1931   Gadamer's *Plato's Dialectical Ethics* is published in Leipzig.

1934   He is appointed to the chair of philosophy at the University of Kiel.
        The circumstances of the appointment are not clear, but Gadamer
        replaces the incumbent suspended because of his Jewish origins.

1936   He attends Heidegger's lectures in Frankfurt on the nature of art,
        later published as *The Origin of the Work of Art*. These lectures
        have a lasting influence on Gadamer's understanding of art.

1939   He moves to Leipzig and teaches philosophy at the University of
        Leipzig.

1945   Leipzig is occupied by Russian troops.

1946   After the Second World War Gadamer is elected Rector of the
        University of Leipzig.

1947   He takes up an appointment at the University of Frankfurt in West
        Germany. He is instrumental in assisting the philosopher Theodor
        Adorno secure an academic post in Frankfurt. Adorno had fled from
        the Nazis in the early 1930s, first to Britain and then the United
        States, where he spent the war years.

1949   Gadamer takes up an appointment of professor at the University of
        Heidelberg where he stays for the rest of his life.

1950   He marries his second wife, Käte Lekebusch.

1956   His second daughter Andrea is born.

1957   Gadamer is invited to give the Cardinal Mercier lectures at the
        University of Louvain. The lectures, entitled 'The Problem of
        Historical Consciousness', contain the central ideas of what was to
        become *Truth and Method*.

1960   The publication of *Truth and Method*.

1967   The publication of the first volume of the collected shorter works (*Kleine Schriften*) of Gadamer.

1971   *Hegel's Dialectic: Five Hermeneutical Studies* is published.

1975   The first publication of an English language translation of *Truth and Method*.

1976   The collections of essays *Hegel's Dialectic: Five Hermeneutical Studies* and *Philosophical Hermeneutics* are published in English.

1977   The publication of the autobiographical work, *Philosophical Apprenticeships*.

1980   The publication of *Dialogue and Dialectic: Five Hermeneutical Studies on Plato*.

1981   He debates with Jacques Derrida at the Goethe Institute in Paris. He publishes *Reason in the Age of Science*.

1983   *Heidegger's Ways* is published.

1986   *The Relevance of the Beautiful and Other Essays* is published.

        The first volume of the 10 volume *Gesammelte Werke* (*Collected Works*) is published. The other nine volumes are issued over the next nine years.

1992   *Hans-Georg Gadamer on Education, Poetry, and History: Applied Hermeneutics* is published.

1994   *Literature and Philosophy in Dialogue: Essays in German Literary Theory* is published.

1996   *The Enigma of Health: The Art of Healing in a Scientific Age* is published.

1997   *The Philosophy of Hans-Georg Gadamer*, a volume in the prestigious 'Library of Living Philosophers' series, is published.

2001   The terrorist attack upon the World Trade Center in New York takes place. Asked to comment on this event Gadamer responded with 'the world has become quite strange to me' (as translated in Grondin's biography of Gadamer). This suggests that it is an event he can make no sense of, suggesting that for all the optimistic possibilities in his hermeneutics, this is possibly a point at which no dialogue is possible.

2002   Gadamer dies in the hospital in Heidelberg at the venerable age of 102.

* Much of the information in this section comes from *Hans-Georg Gadamer: A Biography* by Jean Grondin (see Bibliography).

A–Z Dictionary

(NB: **TM** in the text refers to *Truth and Method*, trans. Weinsheimer, Joel and D. G. Marshall, Second revised edition, London: Continuum, 1989.)

—A—

Adorno, Theodor (1903–1969) German philosopher and critical theorist who escaped to the United States during the years of the Second World War. Gadamer was largely responsible for Adorno's return to Germany in 1947, and he helped him secure an academic post at the university in Frankfurt during the former's tenure at the institute. In 1950 Gadamer and Adorno took part in a radio broadcast to commemorate fifty years after the death of **Friedrich Nietzsche**. Despite Adorno's hostility to the fundamental ontology of Gadamer's teacher **Martin Heidegger**, as articulated most explicitly in *The Jargon of Authenticity* (1964), many salient points of agreement between the two theorists can be discerned. Both Adorno's *Negative Dialectics* (1966) and Gadamer's **philosophical hermeneutics** attest to the mutual influence of Hegelian dialectics on their respective projects; however both theorists eschew the teleology of **Hegel**'s system in favour of the historicality of understanding. The shared emphasis on the contingency of understanding evinced in both theorists a re-orientation of philosophical inquiry towards interpretation in order to avoid a relapse into idealism, which in turn elucidates the centrality of the truth–disclosing potential of art in both their theories. As one of the most prominent members of the Frankfurt School for Social Research, Adorno's project was motivated by an analysis of the degenerating effects of reason within society and the concomitant critique of instrumental reason as manifested in the reduction of meaningful experience, a sentiment shared by Gadamer's reproach of **positivism**. The proximities between Adorno and Gadamer were intended to be explored in a dialogue between the two theorists that Gadamer wished to initiate. However Adorno's death in 1969 prevented this from occurring.

Aesthetics   This is the branch of philosophy which studies the nature of art and the beautiful. The word derives from the Greek *aisthēsis*, meaning 'sensation' or even 'sense-perception' because, in one view, art invokes pleasurable or unpleasant sensual responses in the recipient. Although a philosophical interest in the nature of art goes back to **Plato** and the Greeks, the term aesthetics is actually relatively recent, being coined by the German philosopher **Alexander Baumgarten**. Gadamer's work has a good deal to say about the philosophy of art although he is critical of the aesthetic theory of **Immanuel Kant** and its legacy. Gadamer's major works on aesthetics are in Part One of ***Truth and Method***, and the essays in the collection entitled ***On the Relevance of the Beautiful***. Although Gadamer is mainly concerned with the literary art forms, especially poetry, he also writes extensively about the aesthetics of music and the visual arts.

Aesthetic consciousness   To speak of aesthetic consciousness is to suppose that there is a purely aesthetic way of viewing the world, or alternatively, that there is a specific realm of experience we may term the aesthetic. For example, one might say that a piece of music does nothing more than stir up sentiments of well-being or sadness; such a belief reduces music to an aspect of aesthetic consciousness. Running in tandem with this idea is the assumption that there is such a thing as a purely aesthetic judgement, lacking cognitive content, and appealing to 'pure' sensation and feeling. Gadamer strongly contests these ideas because he maintains that all works of art are more than just **subjective** responses; works of art make a claim to **truth** and hence are not just sensations or opportunities to experience feelings and emotions. We do not just wallow in the pleasurable feeling an art work gives rise to; a work of art has something to say and seeks to share its **truth** in playful **dialogue**. Art is a form of **truth** and its meaning is not located in the perceiver but in the art object itself and what it discloses.

Aesthetic differentiation Aesthetic differentiation, a term coined by Gadamer, refers to the idea that a work of art can be understood as being separate from, and irreducible to, the circumstances of its production or its original ceremonial, religious or political context. Other theorists have adopted a similar position by referring to works of art as *sui generis* (existing in a class of their own). Gadamer rejects the elevation of art objects to a separate realm of existence and meaning. Many objects that we now consider to be works of art – religious icons, for example – originally performed ceremonial and other functions and these factors are to be taken into consideration when determining the meaning of a work of art. In fact, for Gadamer, the original significance of art objects is necessarily considered when they are understood hermeneutically. To appreciate an art object in its original non-aesthetic context is what Gadamer calls **aesthetic non-differentiation**.

Aesthetic object For Gadamer, an aesthetic object is not to be treated as a detached entity to be appropriated and understood conceptually. A genuine work of art takes hold of the observer and becomes an 'event' with which we engage. It appropriates, surprises and disrupts the world of the observer by the presentation of an alternative world or an alternative aspect of the present world. An aesthetic object, such as a literary text or a painting, is not that different from other objects in the world: the differences are of degree and not of kind. An aesthetic object opens up an aspect of the world with greater intensity than our encounters with the everyday, but even mundane conversations, for example, are revealing and disclosive, and hence truthful, but to a lesser degree than great art.

Alterity (or 'otherness') Alterity is an important issue in contemporary philosophy. It refers to the possibility that there can be ideas outside a particular mode of understanding or frame of reference that cannot be assimilated by that frame of reference; the radically other refuses to be reduced to something within a familiar frame of reference. The work of the German philosopher **Hegel**, it is claimed by his critics, is an example of a philosophical system where there is an absence of true alterity. His concept of Spirit or *Geist* constantly encounters opposition, but this is ceaselessly absorbed into itself as there is nothing outside Spirit, and the oppositions are ultimately revealed to be aspects of the same thing. Critics of Gadamer detect a similar lack of alterity in his work. Because everything is ultimately **tradition** there can be nothing truly outside the tradition; that is, there is nothing the tradition cannot absorb and make its own. But what if the tradition confronts ideas and thoughts radically opposed or at variance to it? Is it always the case, as Gadamer seems to claim, that the tradition can negotiate reconciliation? Is it the case that the tradition always has strategies for dialoguing with the strange and the foreign? The question is, does the hermeneutical dialogue merely defuse and tame something that is irreconcilable? The argument here seems abstract, but if it is applied to something like culture it may be simpler to grasp. Can we ever really understand a culture other than our own? Is Islam so remote from the cultural reference points of western Christianity, for example, that its fundamental beliefs can never really make sense from without, as it were?

Analytic philosophy   Analytic philosophy, as a distinct movement in philosophy, is relatively recent, but analysis as a philosophical activity is as old as the ancient Greeks. The key figures in the development of modern analysis are **Bertrand Russell**, **Gottlob Frege**, and the early **Ludwig Wittgenstein**. Analytic philosophers tend to use the tools of logic and linguistic analysis to unmask the pretensions of metaphysics, and in this sense they are the inheritors of the empiricist thought of the Scottish philosopher **David Hume**. Modern analytic philosophy focuses upon epistemology and the philosophy of mind and extends these to all aspects of traditional philosophy. Although there are some signs of rapprochement, analytic philosophy has been used as a label to identify those in the philosophical profession who show evident signs of hostility to what has relatively recently come to be known as **continental philosophy**.

Anticipation of Meaning (and Anticipation of Completeness)
In seeking to **understand** (a text, for example), one always anticipates its meaning. At any one time one is focusing on a specific word or a sentence, but at the same time one is also projecting a complete meaning upon the text as a whole; this is the **anticipation of meaning**. This anticipation is one of **completeness**, in that there is an expectation that meaning

will be unitary. But, for Gadamer, the completeness one anticipates is always disrupted by the tension between the anticipated meaning and the resistance from the text, or whatever it is one seeks to **understand**. The tension is more acute when one seeks to make sense of aesthetic objects; the capacity of art works to disrupt anticipations is more evident than our everyday understandings. The anticipation of meaning is another way of describing the opposition between part and whole in the **hermeneutic circle**.

Application The hermeneutic process traditionally involved **understanding** and **interpretation**. Following **Heidegger**, Gadamer adds to this a third element, application. The quest for knowledge and insight is never neutral or impartial, but is always related to the concerns of a specific individual quest. Hence one is always applying understanding to one's self, and because of this all **understanding** is ultimately **self-understanding**. This does not mean that the search for knowledge is little more than self-interested but rather that all knowledge is a matter of concern for the individual enquirer. (See **understanding** and **interpretation**.)

Applied hermeneutics Gadamer's **hermeneutics** is principally concerned with a description of the general task of **understanding** and **interpretation**. Because of the **universal application** of the interpretative process, there is nothing outside the scope of **hermeneutics**. Nevertheless, each aspect of interpretation has its own area of application and specific region of concern. For this reason critics have referred to **applied hermeneutics** as the specific domains of interpretative practice. Gadamer's own interests here concern the application of hermeneutics to **education**, **history**, **medical science**, and **literature**. (See the entry on **philosophy** and Gadamer, 1992.)

Aquinas, Saint Thomas (c. 1225–1274) Aquinas was one of the foremost philosophers and theologians of the medieval period. He was born in Roccasecca in southern Italy and studied in Naples and Paris. He is noted for his scholarship of Aristotle and his arguments for the existence of God in the so-called 'Five Ways'. For Gadamer, Aquinas, like the earlier Christian philosopher **Augustine**, refers to the **inner word** to explain the Trinity and thereby rescues language from the **forgetfulness** he claims develops out of the philosophy of **Plato**. Gadamer's references to Aquinas are to be found in Part 3 of **_Truth and Method_**.

Aristotle (384–322 BCE)   Greek philosopher and student of **Plato**. The philosophy of Aristotle, read together with Plato, was one of the most crucial influences on Gadamer's **philosophical hermeneutics**, insofar as he analyzes the aspects of affinity and continuity that exist between Plato and Aristotle. Moreover, the aspects of affinity and continuity were taken into consideration and developed against the backdrop of the perceived crisis of modernity; that is, Gadamer argues that it is necessary to rediscover and rehabilitate Greek philosophy under the banners of Socratic ignorance, the goodwill that is operative in Plato's dialogical method and Aristotle's articulation of practical wisdom (_phronesis_) in contradistinction to theoretical wisdom (_theoria_). This rehabilitation is carried out with the aim of offering a counterbalance to the unilaterally dominant technico-scientific developments of modern scientific thought. The issue, for Gadamer, concerns the relationship between three dimensions – originally theorized by Aristotle – theory, craft and praxis – and **philosophical hermeneutics** attempts to explore the possibility of characterizing hermeneutics as practical philosophy by reassessing these three dimensions.

Hegel, **Aristotle** and **Plato** represent the fundamental pillars on which Gadamer builds his hermeneutical thought, above all with regard to their emphases on knowledge and understanding in the communally mediated and collective sense. However, Gadamer's hermeneutics importantly appropriates the ethico-political implications of Aristotle's _Ethics_ and, as such, it can be said to be an open rehabilitation of Aristotle's practical philosophy. For example, one need only look at the dialectical rapport between _ethos_ and _phronesis_ upon which Gadamer places emphasis.

Ultimately, Gadamer grafts _phronesis_, understanding grasped as a kind of knowing which can be always otherwise and which leads to the human good, on to the dialogical character of knowledge for Plato, and then subsequently broadens it out with reference to Aristotle's own analysis of the practical good. This analysis of the practical good is shown in the hermeneutic power that expresses itself in the fundamental phenomenon of dialogical understanding, a phenomenon that manifests its essence in the particular structure of _phronesis_.

Importantly, for Gadamer, Aristotle makes the crucial distinction between theoretical and practical knowledge and, by dint of this, practical philosophy is not simply understandable in terms of a general science of the good. Already for Plato, Gadamer argues, a science of the good represents an eminent way of knowing beyond the methods of the sciences of nature. Rather than possessing the structure of knowing proper to craft (*techne*), the phronetic attitude is structured in terms of a way of being or disposition (*hexis* in the Aristotelian sense) that finds its exemplary incarnation in the life of Socrates. This issue has been much debated by interpreters, some of whom have argued that Gadamer, in an attempt to dispel any serious doubts about the differences that exist between Plato and Aristotle, all for the sake of showing the continuity in their conception of shared practical knowledge, has excessively stretched the practical reflection on Plato by interpreting it in the light of Aristotle's ethics at the expense of the latter's equally important metaphysical dimension. It is reasonable to assume that Gadamer does this because of his ambitious attempt to ground Aristotle's philosophy not in the notion of thought thinking itself, but rather in historical finitude and contingency to which hermeneutics bears witness.

More concretely, this can be traced back to the early 1920s – specifically Gadamer's encounter with the phenomenological interpretations of Aristotelian ethics developed by the young Heidegger – and it is also to be found in Gadamer's early work, culminating in his 1930 *Praktisches Wissen*, which is dedicated to the interpretation of Socratic, Platonic and Aristotelian thought. The Aristotelian impulse resurfaces again in the famous chapter in *Truth and Method* entitled 'The hermeneutic relevance of Aristotle', in which Gadamer sheds light on the original relation between the human sciences and Aristotle's moral or practical knowledge. All these developments finally crystallize in the transformation of hermeneutics into a practical philosophy bound up with human existence in an important series of texts written between 1970 and 1980, which find their eventual completion in the translation of the Sixth Book of Aristotle's *Nicomachean Ethics* carried out by Gadamer in 1998.

However, it should be noted that Gadamer does not hesitate to distance himself from Heidegger's interpretations of Aristotle, and he openly dissociates himself from the accusation, which Heidegger makes against Aristotle, of having inaugurated the transformation of philosophy into onto-theology. Such an accusation proves, according to Gadamer, that Heidegger rejects Aristotelian metaphysics in favour of the ontological restructuring of practical philosophy. According to Gadamer, however, an authentic appropriation of Aristotle's ethics cannot take place without an analysis of the intimate relationship that obtains between theoretical philosophy and practical philosophy. Hence Gadamer's position, expressed in *Truth and Method*, emphasizes that hermeneutics not only expresses itself as practical philosophy, but also and above all as hermeneutic ontology. The revaluation of the relationship between metaphysics and ethics opens up a particular reading of the concept of theory in Aristotle, and the relationship that exists between experience and science. The apparent supremacy of the theoretical life for Aristotle does not, according to Gadamer, simply mean the absolute prioritization of the ideal life of contemplation; on the contrary, the contemplative life is not a realizable truth for men, but rests upon and is expressed in our situated love of wisdom. That said, it is possible to point to a potential lacuna in Gadamer's interpretation of Aristotle, insofar as it fails to explain the connection between ontology and theology in Aristotle. The God of Aristotle is without a doubt not a living God in movement, but a separate principle of being which remains central to Aristotle's philosophy.

In many ways, then, *Truth and Method* is dedicated to the nascent hermeneutic insights of Aristotle and the knowledge of the good that is operative in our practical lives. Against the very notion of a pure and disinterested knowledge claim, and the so-called alienation involved in the objective methods of modern science, Gadamer's hermeneutics draws on Aristotle's discussion of the relation between moral being and moral consciousness in order to reinscribe these ideas into the language of situated historical understanding, which is a knowledge of a special kind. Gadamer writes: 'Moral knowledge, as Aristotle describes it, is clearly not objective knowledge – i.e., the knower is not standing over against a situation that he merely observes; he is directly confronted with what he sees. It is something that he has to do' (*TM*, p. 312). Hence, the event of understanding central to **philosophical hermeneutics**, and its Aristotelian lineage, is expressed in the life of action and deed, i.e. it makes itself felt by way of our common and communal *praxis*. That is to say, hermeneutics sets out to trace the process of our acting communicatively through our hermeneutic-linguistic experience that belongs to the dimension of dialogue, both in its contingency and universality.

Art   (See **aesthetics** and **aesthetic object**)

Augustine (354–430 CE) Augustine, also known as Saint Augustine of Hippo, was born in Thagaste, a Roman province in North Africa (now part of Algeria), and is a major figure in the history of philosophy and the history of the Catholic Church. He creates a vital link between the classical and medieval worlds by bringing together Greek philosophy, by way of neo-Platonism, and the tradition of Biblical scripture. After his conversion to Christianity he became an important figure in the Catholic Church and many of his works establish and defend religious orthodoxy. Augustine was also an important figure in the development of **herme-neutics** and his works on the interpretation and understanding of texts – notably in his works, the *Confessions, De Trinitate (On the Trinity)* and *De Doctrina Christiana (On Christian Doctrine)* – are influential and had a profound influence upon both **Heidegger** and **Gadamer**. Of greatest significance for Gadamer is Augustine's account of the Trinity, given in the final part of ***Truth and Method***. In an argument at once complex and enigmatic, Gadamer points to a parallel between, on the one hand, the relationship between God the Father and God the Son, and on the other, the relationship between the **inner word** and the spoken word. The **inner word** (*verbum interius*), a term from medieval scholastic philosophy, refers to a word, thought but not yet spoken, was utilized by Augustine to serve as an analogy for the mystery of the Trinity. Gadamer takes over this idea to show how Augustine inaugurated an account of language that by-passed the more conventional linguistic **Platonism**, whereby words are representa-tional and designative. On the account of language Gadamer inherits from Augustine, he seemingly ignores the implicit Christian theology and affirms a Trinity-like intimacy, not between the Father and Son or Word and Flesh, but between words and things.

Authority This is one of the key terms Gadamer's hermeneutics seeks to rehabilitate. From the time of the **Enlightenment** the notion of authority was treated with immense suspicion: because authority is often arbitrary and sanctioned only by institutional powers, it cannot be legitimated by reason. The thinkers of the Enlightenment were right to question this arbitrary authority, especially when it pertains to the realm of the political, such as the assumed authority in the medieval doctrine of the 'divine right of kings'. Although much authority is illicit, Gadamer thinks it mistaken that all genuine authority must be sanctioned by reason. Controversially,

Gadamer thinks a good teacher has and is an authority not simply by virtue of the power invested in them by the state. A good teacher, with the capacity to draw learners into the conversations of culture, carries his or her own authority. The real authority of a canonical text, for example, is the tradition of which it is a constituent part. Once again, the mistake of the **Enlightenment** thinkers was to reject the learning and scholarship of the past on the grounds that it had no rational justification. An example of this kind of position is to be found in René Descartes's *Discourse on Method* (1637). In the autobiographical Part One of the *Discourse*, he speaks of the dubitable nature of all the works of classical antiquity because they are unable to provide the incontestable certainty he seeks. For Gadamer's hermeneutics, the writings of antiquity do not rest upon self-evident certainty but they have a vital role to play in human understanding, since all understanding takes place within the context of the tradition. The authority of the texts – and ideas – of the past is guaranteed by their location within the **tradition** of the past.

— **B** —

Baumgarten, Alexander (1714–1762)   The German philosopher Baumgarten is best known for introducing the term **aesthetics** to the philosophical lexicon. The term is derived from the Greek word for feeling or sensation; thus aesthetics is the realm of the sensuous response to a work of art or nature. Baumgarten influenced the philosophy of art of **Kant**. Gadamer rejects the identification of art with subjective response and the evocation of feeling. (See **aesthetics**.)

***The Beginning of Knowledge* (1999)**   From the 1960s to the 1990s Gadamer produced a series of journal articles on the **Pre-Socratic philosophers**; these were anthologized in 1999 in German, and published in English in 2001. This work is a companion to *The Beginning of Philosophy* but whereas *The Beginning of Philosophy* focused on **Parmenides**, this work concentrates upon the fragments of **Heraclitus**. Another theme in the work is the nature of knowledge in general, rather than philosophy in particular, as it traces the foundations of modern scientific thought back to its origins in early Greek philosophy.

***The Beginning of Philosophy* (1996)** A collection of ten essays based upon a series of lectures delivered in Italian at the Naples Institute for the Study of Philosophy in 1988. Gadamer takes many of the central themes in the work of **Plato** and **Aristotle** and demonstrates the extent to which they have their origins in the earlier **Pre-Socratic philosophers**, notably **Parmenides**. This work is a useful introduction to classical Greek thought. It also gives insights into the way Gadamer utilizes hermeneutics in his interpretation of ancient philosophy. There are also interesting reflections on the historical reception of the ideas of the **pre-Socratic philosophers**.

Being (See **ontology**)

Biblical Hermeneutics **Hermeneutics**, or the art or practice of **interpretation**, has its roots in the interpretation of Holy Scripture. The Bible presented endless interpretative difficulties concerning the correct understanding of what was, after all, taken to be the divine word. Thus hermeneutics has its origins in the specific interpretation of religious texts, and only in the modern period did hermeneutics confront the more general problem of understanding. Other specific aspects of hermeneutics were the legal and literary varieties.

Bildung This German word is difficult to translate exactly; it means, amongst other things, 'culture', 'education' and 'formation'. Gadamer uses the term to describe an all too easily neglected way of describing a process of understanding which reaches back to pre-modern humanistic scholarship. Modernist science emphasizes **method** as the correct procedure for the accumulation of facts and knowledge. The human, as opposed to the natural sciences, operate with an alternative notion, namely, ***Bildung***. Human science is not based upon an accumulation of facts or the testing of theories; rather it is an appreciation of organic development, operating at the level of the individual and society. At the individual level ***Bildung*** is the formation of the person as she or he is drawn into a specific cultural framework and finds her or his own voice and individuality within the larger configurations of culture. The process of socialization, the transformation from the natural to the social, is a movement towards an increasing absorption of customs, habits and traditions. At a broader level, ***Bildung*** is the movement of a culture as its customs and traditions develop historically. Gadamer's real purpose in speaking of ***Bildung*** is to counter the idea that knowledge and its accumulation is a process in conformity to a strict and precise method, revealing certainty and precise truths. On the contrary, human understanding is what happens within the process of ***Bildung***.

—C—

Celan, Paul (1920–1970) Paul Celan was the *nom de plume* of the poet Paul Antschel. He was born to Jewish parents in Czernovitz, Romania in 1920. The family were exiled to labour camps in the Ukraine where Celan's mother was shot and his father died of typhoid. In 1948 he moved to Paris, where he worked as a poet and translator. He drowned himself in the Seine in 1970. Gadamer produced a commentary upon Celan's poetic cycle, 'Breath turn' (*Atemwende*) or 'Breathcrystal' (*Atemkristall*).

The 'Classical' When speaking of 'the Classical' one usually contrasts it with 'the Modern'; the classical here refers to the intellectual production of the ancient world, specifically the world of Greek and Roman culture. Critics have taken Gadamer to task for having too much reverence for the ancient world and for endowing it with some kind of metaphysical priority to the modern world. Although much of his work involves interpretation of ancient texts, and although he uses the notion of the classical to defend his version of hermeneutics, Gadamer rejects the criticisms made against him. He claims that his use of the classical stems from an everyday use of the term. When we speak of a film or a book as a classic, it means we are drawn back to it time and time again. The classical is a form of the classic. It is a model of the hermeneutical transaction, for despite the **historical distance**

between the classical text in the past and the interpreter's horizon, it still maintains its significance and continues to make a claim upon the present.

'Closed circuits of historical life'   Referring to the idea of the individual subject in *Truth and Method*, Gadamer is somewhat dismissive of a traditional notion of the self. It is not that he rejects **subjectivity**, it is that he dismisses the 'ghost in the machine' idea, perpetrated by **Descartes**. Our life, that is our 'historical life', is to be understood as a dimension of the broader structures of the family and society, and not the introspection of a mythically given self. When Gadamer speaks of 'closed circuits' it seems as though we are little more than dimensions of the actually existing aspects of historical life, such as family and society. This begs the question: does Gadamer, in his attack upon the Cartesian subject, go so far as to annihilate subjectivity entirely, in the sense that we are no more than unwilling fragments of a broader historical framework? (See **subjectivity**.)

The 'Cogito'   (See **Descartes**.)

Collingwood, R. G. (1889–1943)   Robin George Collingwood was professor of metaphysics in Oxford. As well as a philosopher, writing on philosophical method, metaphysics and art, he was also a notable historian, of Roman Britain, and a practising archaeologist. His awareness of the inescapability of the past had a marked effect upon his conception of philosophy. He was highly critical of his Oxford contemporaries for whom historicism and the history of philosophy were unimportant. They took language and logic to be timeless features of our understanding. Collingwood is critical of an over-dependence upon formal logic and offers in its place an alternative logic, sensitive to context, which is a procedure for understanding and interpreting both historical events and historical texts. This alternative logic he termed a **logic of question and answer**. In essence, this logic does not consider the formal properties of propositions but considers the motivation behind a statement. Collingwood operates on the assumption that all statements are ultimately answers to questions, and the task of the philosopher, not unlike that of the historian, is to uncover the question to which the statement, is directly or implicitly, an answer.

Collingwood's **'logic of question and answer'** had a marked effect upon Gadamer. He takes from this the idea that hermeneutical understanding

gives priority to questions rather than answers. This means that in interpretation one should see the task as fundamentally uncovering an answer to
a question, rather than analysing an assertion. The task of unravelling the
question or questions motivating philosophical texts is as much a historical
task as a philosophical one. (See '**logic of question and answer**'.)

Concept and 'concept history'   As a corrective to **problem history**,
the idea that the history of philosophy is no more than a set of responses
to a stock of specific problems, '**concept history**' ('*Begriffsgeschichte*')
sought to overcome some of its antecedent's theoretical difficulties by
paying closer attention to historical context. Straddling philosophy and the
history of ideas, this position tracks the development of leading concepts
as they appear and, in most cases, develop, in historical texts. Conceptual
history is alert to changes in semantic applications, thus demonstrating the
implausibility of 'problem history'. Gadamer uses the example of freedom
to show how there is no abiding 'problem ... but a complex history to the
way the notion ... is conceptualized.' 'Does it make sense to speak of the
identity, the sameness, of the problem of freedom', he asks, 'in such a
way as to suggest that this problem could ever arise in any other way than
as a constantly new, vital reasons calling into question ... the actuality of
freedom?' He continues: 'Plato (does not defend) the ability to act freely at
any given moment – rather, he was mythically establishing the individual's
responsibility for his life as a whole. It is obvious that this in turn implied a
different sense of freedom than did the Stoic retreat to that which is within
our power. It is also obvious that neither the Platonic nor the Stoic problem
of freedom, nor the problem of freedom of a Christian, has anything to do
with ... determinism in modern natural science' (Gadamer, 1986c, p.2). For
many years the historical analysis of concepts became a major force, not
in academic philosophy but in the interdisciplinary domain of the history
of ideas, in both the Anglo-American world and Germany. Significantly,
Gadamer's hermeneutical slant on concept history is quite unlike that of
many of his contemporaries and differs from the Collingwood-inspired,
and more empirically minded, work of the Cambridge historian of modern
political thought, **Quentin Skinner**. At the same time he remains at a
distance from his compatriot and former pupil, the father of recent German
conceptual history, **Reinhart Koselleck**; this despite the fact that Gadamer
founded with him in the 1950s a journal for the study of **concept history**.

Gadamer's pursuit of a hermeneutically guided history of concepts is adumbrated in a much neglected but revealing short essay, 'The history of concepts and the language of philosophy' (Gadamer, 1986c). Here Gadamer is specifically interested in the concepts of philosophy whose fate, he claims, is quite unlike that of (natural) science. Science may adopt the words and concepts of everyday language but a specialist and technical – and often precise – sense is imposed upon the terms, removing them from associations with pre-scientific origins. This is not the case with the concepts of philosophy where the language of the everyday, however hard one might try to make it otherwise, is constantly in play and may be ignored and silenced but never entirely banished: this state of affairs has important consequences.

In the 1986 essay Gadamer gives the example of the transformation from the Greek word hypokeimenon to the modern concept of the '**subject**' and '**subjectivity**'. *Hypokeimenon* is usually taken to mean substance in Aristotelian philosophy but a more literal translation would be simply 'that which underlies something'. This was later translated as the closely associated Latin term, *subjectum*, literally *sub-jectum*, or 'that which is thrown under'. This in turn eventually becomes the *ego cogito*, and the modernist Cartesian concept of '**subjectivity**' is consequently inaugurated.

Gadamer seeks to go a stage beyond the mere swapping of one concept (substance) for another (subjectivity) by suggesting that the pre-conceptual *hypokeimenon* points back not to a prior concept but to an ordinary everyday word without philosophical – that is, conceptual – associations. In this case Gadamer suggests such vocabulary derived from the practical context of work. The connection with and influence of **Heidegger** here is evident.

Conservativism For many critics there is something intrinsically conservative about **philosophical hermeneutics**. The reverence for tradition and the unwillingness to engage in critique are, for Gadamer's opponents, evidence of a failure to escape or oppose the conceptual and political confines of the cultural status quo. This has also led critics to view Gadamer as a political conservative. Against this Gadamer has always identified himself as a liberal democrat rather than a conservative. Like **Heidegger** and **Wittgenstein** he embraces a politics of cultural critique deriving from

Nietzsche, which rejects the foundations of industrial society and the rule of technocracy and scientific rationalism. (See **John Stuart Mill**.)

Contemporaneity   A Kierkegaardian concept that is developed in *The Philosophical Fragments* and refers to the possibility of grasping or living the truth of Christianity as opposed to accessing it via speculative and historical methods. With this concept Kierkegaard wants to show that there is no mediation between the contemporary believer and God becoming man that can be given by reason or historical evidence, i.e. in terms of a hermeneutics of sacred texts. Rather, the only way to confront the Christian truth is to become contemporaneous with Christ and to face the scandal and absurdity of the paradox of Christ's human and divine nature in the same way that the apostles had to confront the God-man. With this notion Kierkegaard is attempting to subvert our immediate and unexamined belonging to the Christian tradition, a belonging that was taken for granted by his own contemporaries. Kierkegaard also has in mind here the coming together of the eternal and the temporal, in believers becoming contemporaneous with Christ in participating in the event of redemption. What is important is that historical mediation, i.e. the mediation of historical texts or sources, is insufficient when it comes to a bringing together one's own present and the redeeming act of God becoming man. Becoming contemporaneous, then, is the genuine participation in the redemptive event itself.

Gadamer's interest in the concept of contemporaneity is less oriented towards religious truth than it is to the aesthetic experience of truth and the temporality of aesthetic experience. Here Gadamer focuses on the participatory quality of the artwork broadly construed, and emphasizes that becoming contemporary with that which has a strangeness to it is not the same as becoming familiar with the original intentions of the work's creator: it is not an ideal transportation back to the creator's motivations or aims. As Gadamer writes, 'To understand [a work of literature] does not mean primarily to reason one's way back into the past, but to have a present involvement in what is said. It is not really a relationship between persons, between the reader and the author (who is perhaps quite unknown), but about sharing in what the text shares with us. The meaning of what is said is, when we understand it, quite independent of whether the traditionary text gives us a picture of the author and of whether or not we want to interpret it as a historical source' (**TM**, p. 393). Thus the key operative notions here are communal participation, conversational engagement and **application** when it comes to encountering a text or an artwork so that one can become contemporaneous with it, let its past speak to your present, and let the temporality to which it belongs, no matter how distant or strange, break in on the temporality of our understanding. Becoming contemporaneous is thus a task for historical consciousness, 'a task and an achievement that is demanded of it. It consists in holding on to the thing in such a way that it becomes "contemporaneous" …' (**TM**, p. 124). In a word, what is at stake in Gadamer's account of contemporaneity is the task of mediating between the contemporaneity of the living present and the presence of our historical cultural heritage.

Continental philosophy (see also 'analytic philosophy') Contemporary philosophy is frequently divided into 'continental' and 'analytic' traditions. This is a fairly specious distinction, readily challenged, but in the minds of many it represents a rigid divide between two distinct conceptions of the philosophical project. Analytic philosophy grew out of the tendency within positivistic and empirical thought to ally philosophy to the methods and procedures of natural science. In the twentieth century analytic philosophy aimed at a procedural precision by analysing the logical structure of argument, and a consequent concentration upon the use and structure of language, at one time referred to as 'linguistic analysis'. Combined with this is a quasi-scientific concern for the nature of mind as the key to determining the nature and limits of human knowledge. The focus on precision and objectivity inclines analytic philosophy towards the procedures of natural science and away from the more interpretative and historically based humanistic sciences. Those who lay the foundation stone of the modern analytic tradition are the early modern British empiricist thinkers **John Locke**, **David Hume**, and **John Stuart Mill**.

Continental philosophy, as the name suggests, works within the mainstream of philosophy developed on the continent of Europe, hence its alternative name of 'European philosophy'. Many of the leading lights of continental philosophy worked within the European continent – mainly in France and Germany – but at the heart of their work is less a commitment to a geographical region than to a set of philosophical procedures and concerns. Modern continental philosophy generally starts with **Immanuel**

Kant, G. W. F. Hegel and **Friedrich Nietzsche** as the initiators of many of the later concerns. In the twentieth century the key figures are **Edmund Husserl, Martin Heidegger** in the German tradition, and **Jacques Derrida, Emmanuel Levinas, Jean-Paul Sartre** and **Michel Foucault** in the French tradition.

To oversimplify things slightly, it could be said that whereas analytic philosophy is guided by the procedures of the natural sciences, continental philosophy is guided by the concerns and procedures of the human sciences. To oversimplify things even more, we could say analytic philosophy sees itself as a science and continental philosophy is more inclined to see itself more as an art (although there are obvious exceptions). But the difference between these two approaches to philosophy is not just methodological and procedural. Continental philosophy is concerned to understand and describe the character of human existence, and it focuses in detail upon the character of lived experience. There is also a strong commitment to a philosophical understanding that is historical and respectful of the traditions of the past. With these factors in mind it is easy to see how Gadamer is clearly within the continental tradition. It is also evident when one reads his work that because his reference points of **Hegel, Husserl** and **Heidegger** (continental philosophy's 'Big Three'), he is little concerned with the work of the analytic tradition. Nevertheless, in recent years analytic philosophers have come under the influence of hermeneutics generally and Gadamer in particular; one thinks of the work of **Richard Rorty, John McDowell** and **Donald Davison**, for example. On the other hand the close connection between Gadamer and one of the founding fathers of the modern analytic movement, **Ludwig Wittgenstein**, has received some attention of late. What brings these philosophers together is their stress upon the centrality of **language** but they approach it in different ways, bringing out the continental/analytic opposition.

No doubt Gadamer would have found difficulty in speaking of rival **traditions in philosophy**. He would have been at pains to emphasize the unitary nature of the discipline; there are not separate traditions but one all-encompassing **tradition** with differences of emphasis and perspective. It is the commonality of the western **tradition** itself that would provide the basis for a rapprochement between the frequently antagonistic 'continentals' and 'analytics'.

Critique of ideology   (See **Habermas**, **Gadamer-Habermas debate**, and **Ideology critique**.)

—D—

Deconstruction   Jacques Derrida introduced the term 'Deconstruction' in *De la grammatologie* (1967) as an attempt to translate Heidegger's terms *Destruktion* and *Abbau*. In this context, both terms are concerned with analysing and subverting the structures of the traditional ontological concepts underpinning Western metaphysics. As such, Deconstruction questions the philosophical tradition in an attempt to understand how it is constituted as a metaphysics of presence, a metaphysics that takes its start from an understanding of being and beings as extant entities.

From this perspective, Derrida introduces a neologism – *différance* – that focuses on the dynamic nature of difference, an irreducible condition of the possibility of self-identical presence. According to Derrida, identity or self-sameness is not something given, but is rather determined in relation to the other, which endlessly differentiates itself from itself. It is from this differential and self-differentiating dynamic that we must think of oppositional distinctions that constitute the conceptual field of metaphysics and their intelligibility. Importantly, there is nothing mysterious in the concept of *différance* (Derrida even claims that it is not a concept!), insofar as it displays an adherence to the discussion of 'absolute difference' in Hegel's *Science of Logic*. However, Derrida does not follow Hegel's path that leads to absolute knowledge and to the overcoming or sublation of difference or otherness. For Derrida, difference, otherness, or the condition of identity itself, is irreducible to identity thinking. In short, *différance* accounts for the presence of meaning, it accounts for the conditions of possibility of the presence of what is present as meaningful, but in its self-deferral it does not allow itself to be present. Deconstruction is therefore something that is always already at work, irrespective of the willing and wishing of various interpreters or thinkers. Even if Derrida often refers to Deconstruction as a strategy of reading, it is, however, not a method to be used and applied to texts, mainly because it is not a technique which can be applied from without, but rather an operation which is always already at work within the text. Ultimately, Deconstruction aims to demonstrate the radical instability of texts in such a way that they undermine and fail to sustain their own most fundamental categories. Derrida is at pains to demonstrate the radical instability of meanings and categories. (See **Derrida**.)

Derrida, Jacques, (1930–2004)   French philosopher and the founder of a movement known as **Deconstruction**. In his 1989 reply to Jacques Derrida, Gadamer argues that it is very difficult to know what Deconstruction is and what Derrida means when he accuses **philosophical hermeneutics** of being a philosophy that aims wilfully to control and subjectively to domesticate meaning. For instance, in the case of understanding, according to Derrida, hermeneutics seeks to take ownership of and control the nature of meaning in the very act of understanding and, for Derrida, this form of understanding is linked to the history of metaphysics in its attempt to dominate the given of experience. In the same reply, Gadamer emphasizes that since Plato's time the dialogue of question and answer has served not only to reach common agreements, but also to eliminate false agreements, misunderstandings and misinterpretations. Gadamer concludes, ironically it must be said, by excusing himself and his inability 'to understand' Derrida's criticism. For Gadamer, the individual can never know in advance what he or she will discover about himself or herself (and the matter itself) in the play of question and answer. The same can be said, then, about attempts to understand nature. Hermeneutics does not set out to control nature, but to listen to it and to understand it as other or alien so that the interpreter can emerge transformed from such an encounter. Derrida, on the other hand, believes that this attempt to understand other cultures, life-worlds and nature leads to difference being assimilated, flattened out and absorbed in the very act of appropriative understanding. However, this is not what happens because, as Gadamer emphasizes, the hermeneutic struggle to recognize oneself in the Other is all about finding a home amidst the strange – this is the basic movement of a being which consists in a return from self-otherness.

For Derrida, however, any assumption of the continuity of meaning is regarded as metaphysical. In contrast, the entirety of Gadamer's work has been directed towards recognizing the other and otherness, the other as other, in the work of art and in the presumed communality of understanding, without which human existence would be reduced to an unintelligible speechlessness. However, Derrida believes that Gadamer has conceded too much in his search for mutual understanding and agreement. For Derrida, this process ultimately leads to the continuity of meaning, and consequently to what he sees as hidden metaphysical structures that are operative in the philosophical language we use. In his 1989 Letter to Dallmayr, Gadamer answers these criticisms by asking what exactly does the 'language of metaphysics' mean. 'Language', Gadamer writes, 'is always simply that which we speak with others and to others. If we are speaking in another language than our own, *it is again something that is spoken with others* and in which I have to listen to others' (*Dialogue and Deconstruction*, 98). Hence, the nature of language in Gadamer's philosophy means that 'Philosophy must give ear to an older wisdom that speaks in living language' (ibid. 99). This is precisely the case because the Greek language of philosophy has always been the language of conversation; however, the experience of conceptuality for the Greeks, and its eventual transposition into Latin, resulted in alienation and the weakening of the conversation model. Heidegger suggests that this alienation can be challenged and exposed by what he calls *Destruktion*, a methodological concept developed in order to break the fixity of a lifeless or bloodless concept. The goal of the *Destruktion* is to let philosophical terms speak and breathe again in the living language of dialogue. It is important to note that this is not the same as arguing that we should return to an original meaning or truth. According to Gadamer, Derrida's claim that **philosophical hermeneutics** is logocentric reveals an inability to accept the genuine potential of the word *Destruktion*. Destruction may sound threatening, yet it carries no such negative connotations, Gadamer tells us. *Destruktion* is an unbuilding or dismantling, an unbuilding or dismantling of what has been covered over by layers of sedimented metaphysical meaning. Gadamer acknowledges that he is following in the footsteps of Plato with regard to the manner of philosophizing. However, he argues strongly that this does not imply a return to the perceived logocentrism of Greek thought because the lyrical power of Plato will always brings each and every reader into a new present and into a new relationship with that present. Gadamer argues that Plato himself was also applying a dismantling methodology to his own inherited concepts and Derrida's deconstruction, and its subverting tendencies, is unable to turn its back on this history.

Gadamer makes this particular statement about *Destruktion* because he believes that with the spread of the word *Destruktion* in other languages, it has gradually acquired the negative tone of devastation that it originally did not have. In particular, this criticism is made against Derrida, who, according to Gadamer, hears in the word 'destruction' (*Destruktion*) only 'demolition' (*Zerstörung*) (ibid. 121), thus following a path from *Destruktion* to deconstruction which misapplies Heidegger's concepts of *Destruktion*, *Überwindung* and *Verwindung*, which were designed to breathe new life into Greek thought and to let it speak its truth again.

It is with these very elements and arguments that Gadamer's philosophical hermeneutics enters into a conversation with **Deconstruction** concerning the nature of language and texts, and, more specifically, about the interpretation of these texts. The 1981 symposium, held in Paris, the proceedings of which were edited by Philippe Forget in 1984, was published as *Text and Interpretation*. This text generated several other texts on the same topic. Gadamer's concern was to position himself in relation to deconstruction, and soon after the publication of *Text and Interpretation* there followed 'Destruktion und Deconstruction' (1986), 'Fruhromantik, Hermeneutik, Dekonstruktivismus' (1986), and more recently in the complete works of Gadamer 'Hermeneutik auf der Spur' from 1996. The 1996 text was Gadamer's last word on the issue.

One of the key aspects of the dispute between Gadamer and Derrida emerged from the meeting in Paris in April, 1981. Derrida criticized Gadamer's unconditional appeal to the communality of the goodwill to understand, stating that, after all, behind such a 'good will' there is concealed the Nietzschean 'will to power' and that therefore this discourse would lead to a relapse into a metaphysics of the will. To these objections, Gadamer responded by simply noting the undeniable dialogical evidence which is based on the fact that the one who opens his/her mouth – including Derrida and other proponents of Deconstruction – wants to be understood, otherwise they would not speak or write. Gadamer notes the inescapability of the good will to understand, the wanting to say and wanting to be understood, that elementary principle of inter-subjective communication, which remains true even for those who intend to subvert it in order to search for and uncover the submerged condition of meaning. Thus Gadamer seems somehow to make use of Derrida against the classical sceptical strategy that aims to uncover the contradictory position by opposing it and thus refuting it. On this issue of the will, Gadamer also refuses to accept the fact that he is operating with a Kantian or Nietzschean conception of the will and instead invokes Platonic goodwill as his genuine inspiration.

An important question to ask is: What do Hermeneutics and Deconstruction really want to say? What is common to both? The answer one could offer here points to their joint appeal to the liberation of language from rigid and solidified meanings, and this is nowhere more evident than in the permanent play of language. For Derrida, the text is always open to a multiple play of meanings, due to the operation of the language in which *différance* plagues the sign. And the sign, both in spoken discourse and in the written word, does not work as a sign without referring to another element which is not present. This interplay of signs within language means that language is not simply present or absent, but rather exists differentially. In this connection, the nature of language and its metaphysical residue is incomprehensible except as something that needs to pass repeatedly through the sieve of Deconstruction.

In 'Destruktion and Deconstruction', Gadamer finds himself bound to Derrida, since both are engaged in the same project – dismantling the language of metaphysics. However, Gadamer sees the concept of text or textuality as what unites and separates both thinkers, and Gadamer asks the question as to whether language is a bridge or a barrier. For Gadamer it is not possible to reach a static concept of the text insofar as it is continuously impacted by new voices. The text always remains in front of us, speaking with a new voice and challenging us again and again. What is necessary, so as not fall back into misconception, is to consider reading and interpreting as the hermeneutical task of transforming the texts and bringing them back to the living word. Interpretation, therefore, is what brings writing, speech or petrified meaning back to life in and through dialogue. It is an event capable of overcoming the potential self-alienation of writing. Speaking is a dialogue, an effort that continuously modifies itself, and as such it leaves behind the apparent simplicity of the speaker's intended meaning, and consequently the return is the hermeneutic event of speaking in a new voice and the text is but one phase in the communicative event. That said, the question arises: Is the criticism that Derrida levels against **philosophical hermeneutics**, i.e. that it falls back into a metaphysics of the will in its so-called attempt to dominate nature, justified? The answer to this question is no. For Gadamer one does not find a return to a naive metaphysics nor does one find a wilful self-assertion in the event of understanding and interpretation. On the contrary, in Gadamer's **philosophical hermeneutics** one finds a discussion of the possibility of a dialogue with nature as other and as partner.

Ultimately, philosophical hermeneutics attempts to allow what is alienated by the written word to speak again. Hermeneutics allows what is alienated, what is culturally or historically distant, speak again. However, in any effort to bring something which is closer to us, we must take care not to forget that the ultimate justification for doing this is to bring out what is not only a new voice, but a clearer voice.

Descartes, René (1596–1650)   René Descartes was a French philosopher and scientist. His principal works are *Discourse on Method* (1637), *Meditations* (1641) and *The Principles of Philosophy* (1644). He is often referred to as 'the father of modern philosophy' for he gave knowledge a new rationale and justification by turning against the dominant scholasticism and adopting the procedures and ideas of the new science of his day. Central to his philosophy was the adoption of an indubitable **method**. The so-called **'cogito argument'** is an integral part of Descartes' method. Claiming that most things can be doubted, Descartes systematically calls into question the evidence of the senses and reason and concludes that everything can be doubted apart from the fact that he is doubting. Because doubting is an aspect of thinking, the more he doubts the more he confirms that he is a thinking being, hence *cogito ergo sum*. Because he cannot doubt that he is a thinking thing, he deduces from this that his mental, thinking identity is quite different from his extended, bodily identity; in fact he is made up of two substances that happen to work together (because he is made of two substances his position is referred to as 'dualism'). The mind-body dualism is central to understanding Descartes' philosophy but it is more important to appreciate the centrality of the method he uses to establish his philosophical conclusions. The method he adopts is one that uses the procedure of doubt to establish truths that are beyond doubt and hence certain. One could say that Descartes uses systematic doubt as a way of establishing absolute certainty. Further, Descartes' method, it is claimed, achieved for all aspects of human knowledge the kind of certainty science achieves because his strict method was itself based upon the procedures of scientific knowledge. Method, as conceived by Descartes and his followers, is the acid test for all true knowledge claims, whether they be scientific or otherwise. The tradition of hermeneutics contests this idea that genuine knowledge depends upon the adoption of an indubitable method. This is especially true of Gadamer's **philosophical hermeneutics**. (See **method**.)

Dialogue (and conversation)   For Gadamer, understanding is always part of a dialogue. The character of the dialogue has already been suggested in the fusion of horizons, because when horizons interface they engage in dialogue; or at least this is Gadamer's vision. Some may see the coming together of horizons or consciousnesses as the opportunity for gladiatorial combat. They may see the object of the encounter to be the supersession or the obliteration of the Other, whereas for Gadamer under-standing is the accommodation of the Other. This was what was meant by the **fusion of horizons**; the point is not to overshadow and abolish the horizon of the past (conceived as other), but to show how that horizon has been taken up and expanded in the present; this is a question of not exposing the weaknesses of the past such that they had to be superseded by the present, but by bringing out the sense in which the present is just the past in a new form.

Gadamer illustrates his hermeneutics of dialogue by highlighting two aspects from the history of philosophy. His first concerns a radical re-reading of early Socratic dialogue. In these early dialogues Socrates is witnessed doing battle with the leading sophists of the day. Using the tricks of sophistry as much as his opponents he succeeds in silencing many of his interlocutors. The orthodox view of these early Platonic works is that Socrates paradoxically reveals the fragility of truth and knowledge by exposing the limitations of sophistry. He does this by defending a version of absolute truth against the dangerous relativistic sophistry of his opponents. Socrates does argumentative battle with his adversaries, and through the force of hardnosed logic exposes the limitations of weak argument.

Socrates, according to the standard reading, epitomizes the triumph of logic over bogus reasoning. Against this heroic account Gadamer offers another picture. Socrates speaks of himself as a midwife and this self-description fits in well with the Gadamerian interpretation. As midwife Socrates is not in possession of truth but is there at its birth. Like a midwife he is not the central figure but a facilitator. The real birth of truth is what happens in *genuine* dialogue. After all, the early Platonic texts are not treatises but conversations, everyday exchanges, dialogues in the most informal sense. Not only does Socrates facilitate truth, he facilitates dialogue. Socrates, as the purveyor of Aunt Sally arguments he sets up merely to knock down, and Socrates, as the exposer of sham wisdom, pretension and arrogance in his opponents in argument, gives way to an alternative interpretation. Here Socrates is only one voice in a larger conversation where all are participants rather than disputants; he provides the conditions for the emergence of truth from the collective voice of the conversation. **Truth**, whatever it is, can only emerge from dialogue (essentially as conversation with and within tradition). For this reason, the early works of Plato are written in dialogical form, not just because this makes for a stylish and dramatic literary presentation, but because truth is dialogue. There are many things to be said of dialogue that are equally appropriate to truth.

One essential aspect is incompleteness. A genuine dialogue or conversation is characterized by its very lack of completeness and structure. We speak of 'falling into' or 'striking up' conversations, suggesting that they are never planned and just happen. No one knows where they will lead as they are not regulated by rules and conventions and yet they have a kind of structure of their own. Gadamer comments: 'What emerges (in the dialogue) is neither mine nor yours and hence so far transcends the interlocutors' subjective opinions that even the person leading the conversation knows that he does not know' (*TM*, p. 368). He adds that: 'We say that we "conduct" a conversation, but the more genuine a conversation is, the less its conduct lies within the will of either partners. Thus a genuine conversation is never the one that we wanted to conduct' (*TM*, p. 383). Dialogues move in unpredictable directions, unaccountably changing in tone from frivolous to the deeply serious, often leading from something as innocent as a chance remark. And the authentic dialogue reveals something about its participants. Dialogue is the very opposite of self-reflexive, monadic introspective thought. It is intrinsically spoken (as opposed to written or merely thought) and it takes place in a public forum. All these qualities of the dialogue are equally applicable to Gadamer's notion of truth (and his conception of Plato's conception of truth). In the genuine dialogue, the participants change as initial assumptions are challenged, modified, held up to scrutiny in the public court of appeal, in the dialogue itself. It was suggested that the prejudices sustaining understanding could never be made the object of scrutiny. This can be taken as read, but prejudices can rise to the fore in dialogue as they are frequently challenged and surprised in dialogical encounters. This is not a case of raising prejudice to the level of self-consciousness but more a matter of becoming aware of one's funda-mental reference points by having them challenged or taken by surprise. This is not so surprising. A productive dialogue often has the effect of forcing one to see things differently and in a new light. Although Gadamer frequently refers to the importance of **dialogue** in **hermeneutics**, he also speaks of the importance of conversation. The difference between dialogue and conversation is that over time the pure informality of Greek dialogue, as witnessed in the writings of Plato, largely in dialogue form, eventually become formalised in the structured **dialectic** of later thinkers such **Hegel**. (See **dialectic** and **Hegel**.)

Dialogue and Dialectic: Eight Hermeneutical Studies on Plato   This work contains a seminal collection of essays spanning almost forty years and the book deals with such themes as Plato and his relation to Pythagorianism, Socrates and Aristotle, and bears witness to Gadamer's philosophical development. This work includes essays from throughout Gadamer's career, including two early essays, 'Plato and the Poets' (1934) and 'Plato's Educational State' (1942), and a number of the most important later essays, including the 1962 essay, 'Dialectic and Sophism in Plato's *Seventh Letter*,' the 1968 essays, 'Plato's Unwritten Dialectic' and '*Amicus Plato Magis Amica Veritas*', as well as '*Logos* and *Ergon* in Plato's *Lysis*' (1972), 'The Proofs of Immortality in Plato's *Phaedo*' (1973) and 'The Idea of Reality in Plato's *Timaeus*' (1974).

By going back to the Greeks and to Plato's dialogical model, Gadamer attempts to show that the understanding which emerges through dialogue is an ever-emerging and never finished rationality, and the labour of dialectic is by its very nature unfinished and infinite. In dialogue, then, we are always beginning to grasp reason in nature and to see in nature and history the realization or actualization of one and the same reason. However, for Gadamer, this is by no means the mechanical grasping of reason; it does not come about through the Hegelian movement of immanent reason in history, but through the risky, contingent, historical and intersubjective context of the fundamental human drive to bring things to a commonality of understanding.

Gadamer is quite clear that complete understanding is an infinite task, and he emphasizes over and over again the reality of human finitude and the incompleteness of human thinking, which ultimately thwarts any philosophical systematization of reality. As such, Gadamer claims that we are always responding to questions that come from beyond us, from the **matter at issue**. Thus, the inherent contradictions in which reason ensnares itself through language force us or summon us to respond. These contradictions compel us to become clear on what is wrong or right and to make arguments for and against it, and the way out of these dialectical contradictions is via the negativity of going through them by means of questioning and searching. Thus dialogue always calls forth a knowledge that is partial, yet this incompleteness always and necessarily points beyond itself to a yearned for knowledge of the whole.

Dialectic The prominence of the dialectic as it is articulated throughout Gadamer's oeuvre is indicative of many of the fundamental elements of **philosophical hermeneutics**. For Gadamer, dialectical reasoning, as exemplified within the Platonic and Hegelian systems, constitutes a theoretical dialogue between the two theorists which expresses effectively what he terms the 'reflective movement' of the concept. The reflective movement of the dialectic, according to Gadamer, testifies to the self-generating development of the concept. Thus the dialectic as employed in its Platonic and Hegelian manifestations progresses immanently through the movement of its internal logical determinations which represents the 'self-unfolding' of thought. Conceived in this way, the utilization of the dialectic evades any reduction to a formal procedure requiring a foundation, as in Fichte. Rather, for Gadamer, the demonstration of the immanent progression of thought within the dialectics of Plato and Hegel overcomes the subjectivism implied in the positing of basic first principles. The critique of subjectivism accomplished by such a procedure is essential to the hermeneutic principle of the horizon of understanding as transcending the subject, and can thus be found nascent, albeit with some modification, within the Platonic and Hegelian dialectic. The concept of the dialectic as espoused by **Plato** and **Hegel** is thus both central to Gadamer's development of his theory of hermeneutics and also to his insistence on a dialogue with past theorists. Accordingly, Gadamer's interpretation of Plato's work concentrates on the structure of the Platonic dialogues and attempts to work through these as they unfold throughout the texts. The structure of the Platonic dialectic for Gadamer inaugurates the priority of the question which constitutes the requirement of hermeneutics that the subject in the act of interpretation simultaneously questions the **prejudices** of his/her particular **horizon**. The **'logic of question and answer'** at the core of the Platonic dialectic is for Gadamer redeemed in the Hegelian dialectic of thought and being. Hegel's dialectic, *qua* mediation of concept and object, appropriates the fundamental elements of the Platonic dialogue through its insistence on the self-progression of thought in accordance with its objects. This for Gadamer represents a method that is inalienable to the procedure and as such is in accordance with his critique of the abstract methodology of the natural sciences. Gadamer's appropriation of the dialectic, as stated above, must be considered with some qualification. Although Gadamer accepts the immanent progression of the Platonic and Hegelian dialectic, his insistence on the finitude of understanding requires that he reject the teleological presuppositions of the latter theorists. The perennial nature of interpretation and inquiry, that for Gadamer constitutes the dialogical nature of hermeneutics, overcomes the idealist premises of the earlier dialectics, and through this indicates the speculative structure of language, which as the 'horizon of hermeneutic ontology' is unbound by strict formal procedure, but is rather dynamic and self-perpetuating.

Diderot, Denis (1713–1784) French materialist philosopher and novelist, one of the leading figures of the French Enlightenment. (see **Enlightenment**.)

Dilthey, Wilhelm (1833–1911) German philosopher and one of the main exponents of German historicism. In his early work, *Introduction to the Human Sciences (1883)*, Dilthey examined the differences that exist between the *human sciences (Geisteswissenschaften)* and the natural sciences (*Naturwissenschaften*), and acknowledged the importance of **historicality** in the discovery of the internalized influence of external social causes on the objective formation of mankind and the cultural world. Unlike the natural sciences, which seek to uncover the generalized objectivity of the world in its external knowability to man, and which comes to be grasped through an explanation of the phenomena, the human sciences attempt to see the general in the particular by inquiring into the precise nature of mankind in the act of direct historical **understanding**, and the inner structures of lived temporal experience expressed therein.

For Dilthey, the pillars of historical reason are the life of the individual in his or her historical rapport with other externally objectifying subjects and dynamic or structural reason, which is expressed in cultural and social institutions. In *The Essence of Philosophy*, Dilthey argues that philosophy must face up to the mysteries of the world and the lived, historical experience of striving towards universal objectivities in an attempt to make sense of the world and our actions and interactions with other human beings within the world. According to Dilthey, then, philosophy can be defined as an intuitive **understanding** of the world, which has a certain basis in the commonality of art and religion. There are three models of the intuitive understanding of the world: the first is realism, of which positivism is a part, the second is objective idealism, and the third is the idealism of freedom. The universal function of philosophy is that of reassessing the condition of man in front of the world of external human determinations and to uncover the limits of human understanding and interpretation through history, and not through philosophical introspection or reflective inwardness.

With Wilhelm Dilthey, then, hermeneutics undergoes a second phase of universalization, after its expansion in the Romantic period to every form of linguistic communication. This is the period in which positivism reigns, the contrast between the natural and human sciences is radicalized, and the question of truth and the problem of defining 'science' against the backdrop of the contingent experiences within human history becomes most acute. In a word, nature explains (*erklären*) itself and spirit understands (*verstehen*). Consequently, the natural sciences are guided by positivistic laws that enable and guarantee the repeatability of their experiments over time, while the human sciences are the contingent and non-repeatable manifestations of freedom. As such, it is a conflict between the universal and the particular. Originally, Dilthey thought that psychology's approach to the human being could render these distinct views thematic. What followed was a critique of the natural sciences for being unaware that those who do science are always historically situated, not universally situated, leading to a critique of historical reason, asserting the historicity of our human reason which is immersed in life. According to Dilthey, the understanding of spirit, in this moment of thought, can be relived in and through the experience of others (*nacherleben*). Following the criticism of the subjectivism and relativism of understanding, Dilthey abandons his psychology, and hermeneutics is taken as the tool of the human sciences. Ultimately, the hermeneutical task is no longer limited to linguistic expressions but to all other expressions of human spirit. Pre-empting Husserl's own discovery, Spirit is thus not subjective but is rather inter-subjective. The paradigmatic example is given by language: it is an expression of freedom; not an individual freedom, but rather a communal freedom that operates by means of reciprocity. Spirit is also not objective and hence remains free from necessity, as opposed to physical laws. And hermeneutics is the discipline that can discern all the manifestations of culture intersubjectively.

Dilthey's influence on both Heidegger and Gadamer is extremely significant, insofar as phenomenological hermeneutics and **philosophical hermeneutics** recognize the need to break with a purely descriptive, non-participatory transcendental **phenomenology** in the name of a philosophy which can think through the historical situatedness and interpretative context of philosophical thought. Both Heidegger and Gadamer take up and ontologize Dilthey's three philosophical steps: lived experience, linguistic expression and understanding, insofar as understanding is not simply directed at the object which is understood, but also towards the lived experience of understanding and the interpretative expression through which this lived understanding unfolds itself as both individual and historically mediated.

Droysen, Johann Gustav (1808–1884) German historian who, under the influence of **Hegel**, became known for his revolutionary research into the social and political age of Alexander the Great, looking specifically at the influence and achievement of great men. Droysen is also concerned with the entirety or totality of history but, unlike **Ranke**, Droysen does not think that the historian should impartially disappear or be subsumed by the immediacy of world history, i.e. leaving himself out only by contemplating God. While holding on to the distinction between the knowing subject and the perfect knower of divine transcendence, Droysen, a student Wilhelm von Humboldt, believes that the historian must become aware of his role in history and the concrete impact that his nationality, religion and political convictions have on his historical understanding.

Gadamer's interest in the question of history is deeply informed by both Ranke and Droysen and his many references to nineteenth-century historicism clearly bear this out. Ranke and Droysen, while taking their start from an opposition to the philosophy of history, the idealistic nature of Spirit and the a priori construction of world history, continued to refer to the unity and regulative ideality of universal history, assigning to historical consciousness a full self-transparency which ultimately forced them to acknowledge implicitly the concept of absolute knowledge, albeit rooting it in the divine. Gadamer believes that the so-called 'historical school' of Ranke and Droysen, with their concept of historical method, was responding to the approach of the natural sciences, which remained wedded to the ideal of objective and experimental scientific knowledge and based its progress on the application of scientific method, which, for Gadamer, 'consists in rising above the subjective fortuitousness of observation and with the help of method attaining knowledge of natural laws' whereas 'the human sciences endeavour to rise methodologically above the subjective fortuitousness of their own standpoint in history through the tradition accessible to them, and thus attain objective historical knowledge' (**TM**, p. 229).

—**E**—

Education   (See **Bildung** and **free space**.)

'Effective historical consciousness'   (See **'historically effected consciousness'**.)

Embedded self   (See **unencumbered self**)

Eminent text   This is a key concept in Gadamer's understanding of literary texts. Everyday texts – for example, newspapers and reports

– present few interpretative problems, as the meanings they convey are largely unproblematic. Literary texts, by which Gadamer means dramas, novels and especially poetry, are another matter, for their meanings do not disappear after they have been read, as is the case with non-literary texts. The meanings here are literally *e-minent*, that is, they protrude, stick out and make themselves manifest. Gadamer uses the analogy of money to describe the relationship between literary and non-literary texts. Currency is coinage and paper money and, at one time, it was backed up by gold. Coins and paper money have no intrinsic worth or value, they are merely ciphers and representations of that which possesses real value, namely gold. In the same way, eminent texts have real value and everyday language is no more than a simulacrum.

An eminent text also says something about the nature of the artwork and its relationship to its producer. Genuine works of art derive their force from themselves, and language's power of self-presentation, not the author. Here Gadamer is rejecting a romantic notion about the priority of the artist and his or her genius. (See **aesthetic consciousness**.)

The Enigma of Health   Gadamer's work, since the publication of his magnum opus **Truth and Method** in 1960, demonstrates the applications of **philosophical hermeneutics** to specific forms of criticism and education, and in *The Enigma of Health* he focuses upon medical practice. Like the earlier studies in '**applied hermeneutics**', Gadamer illustrates in this collection of thirteen essays the relevance of the central themes in *Truth and Method* to a specific area of practice. One of these themes relates to the origins and consequences of modernity's commitment to a hyper-rational and hence distorted version of the ancient *techne*. Nowhere are these consequences more evident and potentially disastrous than in the realm of everyday practice.

In our scientific age, the forms of practical knowledge, derived through historically conditioned activity, run the risk of obliteration as they get filtered out by a methodized, theoretical world picture. The dangerous legacy of post-Cartesian thought is an intensification of the forgetting of practice we encounter when theory and techne are threatened with merger.

Another important theme from **Truth and Method**, concerning what Gadamer calls **effective history**, that is, the continued effect of the past upon the present, also comes to the fore in this collection of essays. The hermeneutics of effective history, present in all authentic thinking, resists the gravitational effect of attempts to foreclose genuine understanding. *The Enigma of Health* offers a vivid illustration of how these tension-ridden themes work together in the specific arena of medical practice.

The contemporary medical practitioner has access to highly sophisticated technology, whether it be life-support systems, the wherewithal for organ transplantation or computer programmes for diagnosis. A proliferation of research and development has put at the doctor's disposal an endless array of drug therapies. More and more, medical science becomes medical technology as new forms of knowledge are transposed and applied, transforming the doctor into a politically powerful technologist – a technologist of the body. In order to plot the course of this radical change, and to reflect upon its limitations, we need to think through a web of ideas concerning the real nature of technology, its origins in the Greek notion of *techne*, and the connection between *techne and praxis*: this Gadamer does in the first essay in *The Enigma of Health*, 'Theory, technology, praxis'. Drawing upon Aristotle's account of practice in the *Nicomachean Ethics*, Gadamer shows how the 'technologization' of knowledge in the modern world distorts the traditional theory/practice relationship.

For the ancient craftsman, the productive process involved the application of knowledge to a pre-planned object. The artefact emanated from the practical skill (*techne*) of the artisan. Even for Aristotle, the doctor occupied a special place because his practical skill was not directly applied to the construction of an object. Medical art produces nothing in the literal sense: health is not an object. Medicine, and this is one of the central insights Gadamer brings to an understanding of the modern world, can never be reduced to a mere skill. What the doctor seeks to bring about is health, but its return is never a direct consequence of applied skill since skilfulness only relates to the production of artefacts.

Medical practice is, if one thinks back to its primordial sense, the art of healing. Special consideration needs to be given to the terms 'art' and 'healing'. What the modern world is in danger of neglecting is the sense in which the real expertise of the doctor assists (rather than controls) the natural healing process. The doctor requires a special kind of (phronetic) judgement in aiming to restore the essential balance or equilibrium of the patient. The doctor should have no illusions that she is curing the patient with interventionary techniques. At best she can, with solicitude, tentatively apply general medical knowledge to this particular (that is, unique) individual. Medicine is both an art and a special type of skill. The artistry displays itself as the doctor seeks to interpret the imbalance in the patient and guides the process whereby the patient recovers a lost equilibrium. Balance is required of the doctor in that she needs to make a fine discrimination between what will assist the patient and what needs to be left to the 'open domain' of nature. The illness of the patient presents the doctor with a hermeneutical problem.

So easily the doctor's intervention can be fractionally too much or too little, bringing about a complete reversal of the intended effect. Gadamer likens the doctor's art to Rilke's description of the acrobat where, 'the pure too-little incomprehensibly transforms itself, springs over into the empty too-much' (Gadamer, 1996, p. 36). In our scientific age, Gadamer suggests, the fine discriminations of the doctor are limited because technology artificially reduces the necessity for judgment. As Gadamer says, 'the more strongly the sphere of application becomes rationalized, the more does proper exercise of judgment along with practical experience in the proper sense fail to take place' (Gadamer, 1996, p. 17).

The true enigma of health is this. When all is said and done, the doctor is not fully in control, neither is he ever in a position to understand completely the nature of health, the body and healing. The true concern of the practitioner is not the general nature of health but the restoration of the equilibrium of a particular, unique individual in his care. Ultimately health cannot be explained entirely from within the province of the scientific world. 'Illness is a social state of affairs. It is also a psychological-moral state of affairs, much more than a fact that is determinable from within the natural sciences' (Gadamer, 1996, p. 20). More fundamental than general scientific understanding for the doctor is the range of ethical concerns relating to the care the practitioner demonstrates towards the patient and the care the patients exercise upon themselves.

Dialogue, a central feature of understanding, worked out in detail in *Truth and Method*, is at the heart of the doctor/patient relationship. Through dialogue the ethical is made manifest. In discussing what has come to be known as 'medical ethics', Gadamer thankfully avoids the sterile terrain of competing and antagonistic moral principles, so often the generally accepted arena for contemporary philosophical debates, preferring the richer non-theoretical vocabulary of Aristotelian 'virtues'.

The skilled practitioner is not just technically adept but possesses a repertoire of appropriate 'excellences'. A good doctor has 'bedside manner', we might say, especially if we detect trustworthiness, care, co-operation, gentle persuasion and the like. It is in dialogue with the patient that these ethical characteristics come to the fore because only when the patient is in a position to articulate the nature of the pain, discomfort and anxiety can the healing process begin. Good medical practice is essentially dialogical. For Gadamer, general practice is as much concerned with the 'talking cure' as more obviously language-based therapies like psychoanalysis, as he argues, in 'Hermeneutics and Psychiatry' (Gadamer, 1996).

Part of Gadamer's purpose is to illustrate how echoes and traces of words are still – albeit in sedimented form – active and operative in the language of the present. Listening to the reverberations of more authentic meanings, a difficult but not impossible task even in our scientific age, enriches the level of reflection and understanding, making one more mindful of what has been forgotten in a culture's state of collective amnesia. A frequently used example in these essays, because it bears directly upon the medical lexicon, is the notion of 'treatment'. To emphasise the all too easily neglected interpersonal aspects of the doctor's expertise, Gadamer notes in the essay 'Philosophy and medical practice':

> The German word *Behandlung* is a rich and significant word
> for 'treating' people and 'handling' them with care. Within it
> one hears literally the word 'hand', the skilled and practised
> hand that can recognize problems simply through feeling and
> touching the affected parts of the patient's body. 'Treatment'
> in this sense is something going far beyond mere progress in
> modern techniques.

The gap between the methodized world-picture and the hermeneutical openness of effective history will never be closed. The scientific project of the domination of nature, under whose shadow we cower, at least since the 'enlightenment', will never be realized. On the other hand, the increasing tension between technology and ethical life seems to be an ineradicable feature of modernity, although for Gadamer it is a tension we can, like our own health, bring into equilibrium. He says in the Preface to *The Enigma of Health*, '(our problem) is a question of finding the right balance between our technical capacities and the need for responsible actions and choices'. The traditional idea of the family doctor, as both friend and adviser, is supplanted by the anonymous medical technocrat: the patient/doctor relationship makes way for the impersonal domination of experts. Technology is taking over. Yet despite the Brave New World, we can, Gadamer suggests, reclaim the rapidly disappearing forms of collective and personal responsibility necessary to redress the balance without raging against the machine. For this reason, perhaps, Gadamer is reluctant to suggest ways, through an elaborate critique of the structures of modernity, of reversing the alienating effects of change. He refrains from outlining nostrums of political resistance to the inevitable dehumanizing consequences of technology. By the cunning of practice, rather than Hegel's 'cunning of reason', there will always be the opportunity to move within a **free space** uncolonized by the ravages of strictly methodized practice. Despite pressures to the contrary, Gadamer suggests, good practice, medical or otherwise, will always have the resourcefulness ('cunning') to prevent its total annihilation. More than this, good practice, because of its intimate connection to ethical life, depends upon social solidarity, precisely the kind of solidarity we need to develop to resist the excesses of modernity.

The Enlightenment The Enlightenment was primarily an intellectual movement that swept across Western Europe, notably France, England, Scotland and Germany, throughout the eighteenth century. But it was not only a force of ideas as it had vast repercussions for religion, science, technology, politics and the character and nature of social life. In general terms it was a crusade against superstition and tradition, the focus for which was often the authority and power of the church. Many of the thinkers of the French **Enlightenment** were fiercely anti-clerical.

It claimed to base **authority** and legitimacy not on accepted tradition but universal reason, the new litmus test for establishing the credentials of any system of belief or set of practices. The roots of Enlightenment thought are to be found in the so-called New Science, that is, natural science as we now know it, rapidly developing in various centres of activity in seventeenth-century Europe. Galileo in Italy and Newton and Bacon in England established scientific method with its reliance upon reason and observation. The French mathematician and philosopher, **René Descartes**, is a key figure in the formation of Enlightenment thought (even though the heyday of Enlightenment thought was a century after his death in 1650). He sought to give philosophy the kind of foundation and certainty he witnessed in the natural sciences. In part, Descartes is responsible for a key notion in Enlightenment thought, namely, **method**. In contrast to pre-Enlightenment reliance upon the power of tradition, the Enlightenment put forward the idea that adherence to a strict, scientific method would establish reliable and well-founded truths. The key weapon of the enlighteners was reason, against which all claims to truth were to be tested, and if found wanting were to be dismissed. As already stated, the Enlightenment was not simply an intellectual movement that replaced the old authorities of church and state, but a scientific and technological movement: the application of reason to the betterment of human life through a belief in science and progress. The best example of this is the *Encyclopaedia* (*Encyclopédie*). Under the chief editorship of the philosopher **Denis Diderot**, the work comprised 35 volumes, with 71,818 articles and 3,129 illustrations, and it took over twenty years to bring to fruition. Its purpose was to combat the prevailing ideas of the time by casting aside those that were dependent upon superstition, and encouraging individuals to think for themselves with the power of reason. More than this, with its articles on new developments in agriculture, industry and technology, it made new ideas accessible and available to the general public – the literate general public, that is. The self-conscious motivation for the *Encyclopaedia* was to change the way people think.

In 1784 the German philosopher Immanuel Kant published a short article entitled 'What is Enlightenment?' This gives a great insight into a contemporary view, and also offers a succinct account of what the Enlightenment represents. Kant claimed that the motto of the Enlightenment should be *Sapere Aude!* (Dare to know!). He urges his readers to have the courage to trust their own rational faculties and break away from the infancy of thought to assert a new maturity that was self-governing and not dependent upon the authority of institutions. In contrast to the prevailing view that individuals should defer to the established authorities of church and state, he recommends dependence upon one's own intellectual resources. The Enlightenment is not just about the philosophical justification of knowledge, a shift from a dependence upon tradition to the power of reason; it has a strongly political agenda. In daring to know, one at the same time dares to assert one's own autonomy, breaking free from the old political order of the divine right of kings and the **authority** of priests to embrace a new language about individual freedom and natural rights. In many ways the French Revolution and the beliefs that it stood for were a consequence of the ideas laid down by the Enlightenment.

The Enlightenment, in the views of many, was the start of modernity. Modernity, in very general terms, is a belief in the power of progress through the application of reason through science and technology. **Postmodernism**, with its suspicion of a grand narrative of progress, has done much in the last thirty years to question modernism and the basis of the project of the Enlightenment. Although Gadamer's relationship to **postmodernism** is quite complex, he certainly questions the basis upon which enlightenment thought is based. In reviving the notion of **tradition** he aims to demonstrate the ways human understanding cannot be confined to the operation of a strict method.

Epistemology Gadamer criticizes the traditional and dominant scientific model of epistemology and claims that this dominant theory of knowledge undermines forms of knowing that lie outside or even behind this specific methodology. No doubt Gadamer here has nineteenth-century *Erkenntnistheorie* in mind, a theory that came to prominence in the post-Hegelian period. While it could be argued that Gadamer is seeking to rehabilitate a form of knowing which is sympathetic to the those moments of lived insights which lead to new forms of understanding, forms of understanding which are always situated against the backdrop of **effective historical consciousness**, I think it can be argued that Gadamer's thought also incorporates or preserves a theory of knowledge and does not simply jettison epistemology altogether in a way that Heidegger might have. He does this through his various analyses of historically situated and conversational modes of knowing one's way around something, insofar as the knowing which is involved here is not oriented towards an object of theoretical concern, but rather towards a way of knowing which negotiates the particularity and contingency of lived understanding. Like Heidegger, Gadamer too is trying to address the ontological-linguistic ground on which the objectivity of the natural sciences rest and receive their justification: the historicity of the knowing subject. In a word, Gadamer aims to give expression to a form of knowledge experience that is distinct from a dogmatic and self-enclosed epistemic acquisition, a form of experience, a mode of being as 'knowing one's way around', which opens on to a broader and self-enriching understanding of oneself and the other. What makes this mode of knowing valid and immunized against the critique of historical relativism is that Gadamer is at pains to point out that this way of knowing and being is not simply an isolated and self-contained form of existence, but one which is rooted in sociality as an integral element in the process of lived experience, self-correction and human dialogue. This form of knowing, then, is not the knowledge gleaned by an impartial or non-participating spectator, and nor is it a way of being that simply embraces knowing (and by dint of this truth) as historically relative and determined by a given age or world-view. This is precisely why Gadamer, showing his Platonic-Aristotelian predilections, places such an emphasis on the adventure of knowing (the adventure of knowing that we do not know) as a form of seeing, taken together with the curiosity of bringing something new to light which is involved in knowing more than is already familiar. Gadamer even uses our experience of the work of art to underline the presence of curiosity, self-recognition and subjective exploration in the process of knowing more, writing, 'The joy of recognition is ... the joy of knowing more than is already familiar. In recognition what we know emerges, as if illuminated, from the contingent and variable circumstances that condition it; it is grasped in its essence. It is known as something' (*TM*, p. 113). Here Gadamer is trying to bring together the discussion of knowing and the Platonic-Aristotelian concepts of recollection and practical knowing, and what emerges is an understanding which is not theoretical, insofar as the experience of this form of knowledge is inseparably bound up with or confronted by lived experience itself, and is not engaged in an impartial reflection on or thematization of that very experience. One of the reasons motivating Gadamer's discussion of this distinct form for knowing and its Aristotelian lineage stems from the detached objectivity of nineteenth-century historiography which had attempted to uncouple the interpreter and the interpreted in the name of historical objectivity. For Gadamer, then, the hermeneutic situation, in which interpreter and interpreted encounter one another, is determined by the finitude of human experience, and because of this our insight into the hermeneutic situation and our attempts to engage effective historical consciousness are always incomplete. As Gadamer puts it: 'To be historical means that knowledge of oneself can never be complete. All self-knowledge arises from what is historically pre-given' (*TM*, p. 301).

Experience The German word for experience, *Erfahrung*, echoes the etymology of *fahren*, to travel or to wander, and already in Hegel's *Phenomenology of Spirit*, consciousness and its experience are referred to as 'a voyage of discovery'. Many philosophers have interpreted the nature of experience on the basis of the Hegelian concept of *Erfahrung*, and this is particularly present in Gadamer's **Truth and Method**, which echoes the idea of travel as an experience that deeply transforms the traveller, and it is precisely in such an experience that truth exists. The hermeneutic theory of experience is expounded in **Truth and Method** along with the notion of **understanding** (*Verstehen*), highlighting the way in which experience and understanding are always connected and how practical knowledge is acquired by direct evidence from those who have had experience. That is, they are connected insofar as they require active participation, and in this context experience takes on both a cognitive and concrete meaning, which is neither simply epistemological nor intellectual, but rather practical. The use of the Aristotelian category of *praxis*, in fact, goes hand in hand with the resumption of the categories of facticity and life-world – drawn from the early Heidegger and late Husserl – and in this respect, every form of hermeneutic experience is somehow a form of practical knowledge. However, Gadamer emphasizes that the conversion model essential to **philosophical hermeneutics** is a rehabilitation of neo-Aristotelian practical philosophy which leads to an accentuation of the ethical and political implications of Gadamer's thought.

For Gadamer, however, the Hegelian system does not accurately represent the true meaning of the term *Erfahrung*, experience, because the movement within the circularity of consciousness leads one to believe that the experience is enclosed within itself and not open to actual difference or otherness. Indeed, the ultimate goal of Hegel's dialectic of absolute knowledge, where consciousness brings its wandering to an end, is where consciousness rests fulfilled because it no longer needs anything outside itself. But this, for Gadamer, is not genuine experience, because the end is already circumscribed from the very outset and hence the novelty of experience is to a large extent done away with. Only a different and more authentic understanding of experience allows us to overcome the Hegelian system by understanding the finitude of man, a term which indicates not only the experience of the subject, but also the undergoing of a transformation process which is unexpected and which can never be anticipated.

When talking about the experience of truth, Gadamer uses the term *Erfahrung* because of its kinship with lived experience. In general, says Gadamer, we can speak of the experience of truth where there is a real experience, where the encounter with the thing brings about a real change in the subject. The experience of truth is thus an event that moves and displaces consciousness, transforming it in the process. To develop more fully the meaning of experience (which has significant implications for his notion of truth), Gadamer reflects on aesthetic experience, which is understood as one of the areas of human knowledge that has maintained a different relationship with reality, mainly because art was always considered epistemologically poor and thus relegated to the margins as methodologically unscientific. However, Gadamer sees in art a form of extra-methodological knowledge that displays a different relationship with reality and conveys a different sense of truth. But Gadamer's reflections on art have only one purpose, a preparatory one, and they are intended to highlight a model of experience and a different concept of truth from that of the natural sciences.

For example, defining the broader concept of experience is invaluable to a hermeneutic analysis of the concept developed in the context of the play of aesthetic experience. The concept of 'game' frees us from the rigidity of subjective interpretation and is described as a model of experience that reveals the relational structure of being and truth. The game is a means, a medium, and yet the players remain distinct in that the game is not simply created by those who **play** it. Rather, the game guides the players who are taken by the game and who adhere to its rules, adapting to its form. The game therefore has primacy over the players, so we could say that the subject is the game itself, which reveals itself to have a definite identity which is independent of those who play. In a word, in the experience of play, the players are played by the game and not vice versa.

The discussion of the concept of play brings about the weakening of subjectivity and this is Gadamer's way of opening up a new philosophical horizon when it comes to the nature of experience. This is not a move that does away with the notion of actors as players in the game, but rather requires all their skills and their participation if the game is to succeed. Thus the philosophical nature of subjectivity is not to be jettisoned altogether, but rather redefined in its role so that it no longer occupies the centre of philosophical concern.

—F—

Festival   (See *The Relevance of the Beautiful*.)

Forgetfulness (the 'forgetfulness of language')   On Gadamer's reading of the history of philosophy in *Truth and Method*, **Plato** is responsible for downgrading language and making it subordinate to the operations of thought. For **Plato**, thought is more fundamental than language because cognition precedes linguistic usage and thus makes a radical distinction between thought and **language**. Here language is designative because it does little more than name or attach labels to states of affairs, either mentalist or those in the world. This conception of language is found wanting by Gadamer because it is essentially forgetful; forgetfulness is language's failure to be aware of its own being and the fact that it is intimately bound up with worldly affairs and cannot be divorced from them.

Plato is responsible for this account of language. It is in fact the dominant position in philosophizing about language, but there is an alternative position, one mindful rather than forgetful of its own being. This is the tradition out of which hermeneutics speaks and it has its origins in an account of language contrary to the dominant Platonism. Gadamer instances **Augustine**, **Aquinas** and other figures in the scholastic tradition as key reference points here.

Free space   In the modern bureaucratized world, the character of life is managed and regulated by social and political forces over which the individual has no control. Despite this, Gadamer advocates the search for what he terms 'free space'. It is within these spaces, unregulated by experts or forces of the state, that the individual breaks free and searches for the possibility to develop both **solidarity** and autonomy. Higher **education**, despite the tendency for the modern university to become part of the managed and bureaucratized world, offers an opportunity to construct one's own 'free space' in both the solidarity of an academic community and the autonomy of research and enquiry entered into for its own sake and not for the sake of material or financial gain. Here Gadamer clearly endorses the liberal notion of university education as an end in itself and not a means to a further end.

In the 1986 essay 'The Idea of the University' (see Misgeld and Nicholson, 1993), echoing as it does Cardinal Newman's classic defence of liberal education, Gadamer looks to the university as one place where solidarities are preserved and reconfigured. Although the modern university is as much under threat from bureaucratization as is medical practice, Gadamer sees glimmers of hope for the future. The institute of higher education, for all its destructive specialization and cosying up to big business, still offers the chance to discover what he calls a 'free space' which is 'not offered as a privilege to a particular class but as a human possibility.' As well as affording the luxury of the 'free space', the university 'is a place where something happens to us'. He continues: 'This small academic universe still remains one of the few precursors of the grand universe of humanity, of all human beings, who must learn to create with one another new solidarities.' The university, at its best, is a model of a larger solidarity where the spirit of free enquiry and the quest for a 'free space' preserves all that is necessary for the potentially dangerous open dialogue of enquiry and self-discovery. Fanciful, over-optimistic and elitist: these are some of the possible charges levelled against Gadamer's utopian vision here, but his plea for continued independence of mind in the *universitas scholarum* as 'opposed to the moulding of social consciousness by the powers of the present' is clearly relevant to the present day.

Freud, Sigmund (1856–1939)   Austrian physiologist, neurologist and psychologist. As the father of the psycho-analytic school, Freud's influence extends throughout the human sciences and the medical sciences even today. Freud's theory of the unconscious and his tripartite structure of the mind helped lend credibility to the growing distrust of the autonomous ego nascent at the turn of the twentieth century. Freud posited that the mind consists of three levels: the (unconscious) id, the site of our instinctual drives which requires socialization by the super-ego (the site of prohibition on the id), and the (conscious) ego, which is the result of the dynamic tension between the former two levels. Despite Freud's intentions to define psychoanalysis as a purely natural-scientific method of investigation, his description of the unconscious drives governing the id legitimated an almost hermeneutic interpretation of human behaviour. The persistent influence of Freud's theory has extended beyond psychiatry and can be detected in the works of Jacques Lacan and throughout contemporary critical, social and cultural theory.

His key works are: *The Interpretation of Dreams* (1889); *Totem and Taboo* (1913); *The Ego and the Id* (1923); *Civilization and Its Discontents* (1930). (See **hermeneutics of suspicion**.)

'Fusion of horizons' The term **horizon**, occurring as it does in the work of Nietzsche and Husserl, is not a new one in philosophy. In the hands of Gadamer it operates something like Wilhelm von Humboldt's idea that language provides the speaker with not just a means of communication but a standpoint from which to view the world, a world-view. As one acquires the capacity to use language, and as a result of the process of acculturation, one at the same time acquires a '**horizon**', a perspective on the world. The term is particularly appropriate because it suggests a panoramic vista from a particular perspective. As Gadamer says, 'The concept of the "horizon" suggests itself because it expresses the superior breadth of vision that the person who is trying to understand must have' (*TM*, p. 305). The thought here is that to have a horizon is to have a perspective upon the world. This is in part acquired via language; hence the horizon is linguistical in a very basic sense. The power of language to enable one to 'see' and to 'see differently' is alluded to in the idea of the horizon. Language provides the horizon as both disclosure and limit. To be discovered later is the fact that the 'fusion of horizons' is ultimately an aspiration; it can never be fully achieved or finally completed. The suggestion that an easy accommodation of one horizon by the other, with settled harmony and complete agreement ensuing, is very far from Gadamer's intention. Yet despite never achieving total transparency of understanding with the other, the need for interpretation is constant and ever present. Gadamer confirms this when he offers the following: 'The fusion of the horizons of interpretation is nothing that one ever reaches' because 'the horizon of interpretation changes constantly, just as our visual horizon also varies with every step that we take' (Gadamer, 2004, p. 61).

The horizon is not fixed but is constantly changing and modified little by little over time, not by the sheer weight of accumulated experience but by a process of expansion. A 'fusion of horizons' embodies a measure of agreement and this in turn is a partial understanding: '*Understanding is always the fusion of … horizons*' (*TM*, p. 306). The thought here is that a horizon can be brought into contact with another horizon. Instead of one obliterating the other, a process of mutuality or fusion takes place. Gadamer's idea is that this happens both down and across time, that is, diachronically and synchronically. There are many ways to comprehend the metaphor of *fusion* but the most obvious relates to understanding the past, although it includes interpersonal and even inter-cultural understanding.

Is the past another country, even the past of our own language and culture? Certainly things are done differently there, but is it a remote and alien place? And how are those in the present connected to the past? If horizons are in the present how do we connect to horizons in the past? These are some of the unsettling questions Gadamer raises when he evokes the image of the fusion of horizons.

Relativism, the view that there are no objective standards and every perspective is ultimately self-referential, denies the possibility of bridging historical distances. More than time often divides epochs. There are the conceptual difficulties of linguistic and cultural changes making words in the present alien and incomprehensible to those in the past. There are a multitude of problems surrounding the gap between the present and the past at all sorts of levels. Take, for instance, the hermeneutic problem of understanding ancient texts. Aristotle's world is far removed from the present. An ancient term like *eudaimonia*, for convenience sake often translated as 'happiness', and yet quite unlike a modern idea of satisfaction or being contented with one's lot, is just one example of the problem of historical distance. What chance do we have of correctly interpreting Aristotle's texts and seeking to penetrate the lost civilisation of ancient Greece with its manifold practices, beliefs and customs remote from the modern world? Can we correctly interpret the past? It would be a mistaken assumption to refine an interpretative method in such a way that the interpreting subject hits upon the correct interpretation. This would be to repeat the mistakes Gadamer exposed in the scientific method; to transpose this method to interpretation of the past would be mistaken. However, if we were to regard the past as possessing its own horizon, and the task of comprehension for the interpreter in the present is to engage with the 'lost' horizon, then another possibility emerges.

Understanding is not a question of an active subject casting a meaning on an inert and dead object; on the contrary, both the present and the past have horizons that may productively be brought together. The event of understanding is a negotiation of the present and the past; this is invariably linguistic or via an artefact (effectively a language substitute since it stands in need of interpretation). To speak of an ancient text possessing a horizon is to speak of a world-view. The world-view of the past makes a claim, via text, on the present. The ancient text, for all its outdatedness and antiquity, still speaks in its presentation of its horizon. The idea of the fusion of horizons, in some ways explains the nature, and justifies the existence, of the philo-sophical and literary canon. Why do countless generations keep turning back to Plato and Aristotle, Aeschylus and Shakespeare? It is because these texts still have something to say to those in the present. They seek to draw the present into their respective horizons; they seek to draw us into dialogue and they seek to communicate their truths.

But Gadamer is not merely accounting for the possibility of trans-lation and interpretation of ancient texts using established hermeneutical principles; he is providing a model for all understanding. What he also manages to establish is that dislocated subjectivity is a myth. All under-standing takes place from within an embedded horizon but that horizon is necessarily and ubiquitously interconnected with the past. It would be a mistake to say we are always locked into the past, but we are ceaselessly in a present through which the past speaks. This is the character of tradition itself, being made up of past, present and future. Our attempts at self-understanding have a forward-looking element (we are always projecting into the unknown future) but our understandings in the present constantly draw upon, fuse with, the past. The language through which we articulate the present resonates with the meanings from the past and they continue to be operative in the present; this gives a sense of what Gadamer means by '**effective historical consciousness**'.

—**G**—

Gadamer, Hans-Georg (1900–2002)   Hans-Georg Gadamer was born in Marburg in Germany on 11 February 1900 into a middle-class family. His father Johannes Gadamer was at that time a struggling scientist working in Marburg University. Two years later the family moved east to Breslau, now Wroclaw in Poland, where Johannes was elevated to the post of professor. Gadamer's early life was surrounded by domestic tragedy, as first his only sibling, his sister Ilse, died in infancy, and then his mother died from diabetes two years later when Gadamer was four. A year later his father remarried and by all accounts, including his own, he was unable to feel close to his stepmother Hedwig (née Heillich). Gadamer's education at the Holy Ghost School in Breslau was typical for a person of his class and background and his formal education at the Holy Ghost Gymnasium was completed shortly before the end of the First World War in 1918. The same year he matriculated at the University of Breslau and studied, much to the disappointment of his scientific-minded father, a broad introduction to the humanities. This included history, philosophy, literature (mainly German), music, languages and art history. Gadamer's love of the arts and his later decision to work in the humanities was, apparently, a constant source of worry, and no doubt irritation, to Gadamer's rather philistine father. In fact when Johannes was on his deathbed and Gadamer was a philosophy student under Heidegger's tutelage, the teacher was summoned to give a verdict on whether the young Gadamer would make a career of philosophy. Apparently Heidegger spoke well of his promising student at this time, although his opinion was to change at a later stage.

The general education in the humanities Gadamer received played a key part in his intellectual development, for his later influential philosophical work in hermeneutics was, in some sense, an attempt to vindicate and hold on to that ancient idea of education as an initiation into the cultural reference points of western civilization rather than the more modernist notion of education as accumulated specialist knowledge of the sciences. Evidently from an early age the young Gadamer had a passion for literature and the arts generally. Was this a conscious or unconscious reaction to his father's strong commitment to natural science and indifference to the wider culture?

The notion put forward by the historian of ideas, Isaiah Berlin, that all seminal thinkers essentially effect parricide by seeking to kill the ideas of a symbolic or actual father, may be a helpful thought here when seeking to make sense of Gadamer's love of the humanities and snubbing of the sciences. Many critics have accused Gadamer's philosophy of being anti-science. This is an over-simplistic judgement but there is an evident suspicion towards a culture dominated by scientific rationality.

In 1919 Johannes Gadamer received a chair at the University of Marburg and Hans-Georg began studies in philosophy with the neo-Kantian scholar **Paul Natorp** in the same university. He wrote his dissertation on 'The nature of pleasure according to Plato's dialogues' under Natorp. In 1922 Gadamer was afflicted by polio, which swept through Marburg (and well beyond) at this time. He was kept in isolation for many months and used his time profitably reading philosophy: amongst other things he worked through Edmund Husserl's phenomenological classic the *Logical Investigations*; Gadamer was to meet Husserl the following year. The effect of polio was to leave its mark on Gadamer as he was to walk with a pronounced limp for the rest of his life. In 1922, the most important event in Gadamer's intellectual development took place: he met Martin Heidegger in Freiburg. Heidegger was to have a pronounced effect on Gadamer's thinking from this time on, and Heidegger's influence on his future development is profound and far-reaching. Heidegger's reputation at this time, as a charismatic teacher and new voice in philosophy, was gaining rapidly, and in the following year Gadamer moved to Freiburg to attend Heidegger's classes. They struck up a tentative friendship, albeit initially of the master-pupil variety, and Gadamer served as his mentor's assistant first in Freiburg and later in Marburg in the early 1920s when Heidegger took up a new position there. Spellbound by his magnetic teacher, the eager scholar sought to make his mark but was soon rebuffed as his teacher failed to be impressed by his performance. Heidegger made this plain in a letter to Gadamer in 1924 where he made a cutting comment as much about Gadamer's character as about the unimpressive quality of his philosophical work. 'If you cannot summon sufficient toughness toward yourself', wrote Heidegger, commenting on Gadamer's academic performance, 'nothing will come of you' (quoted in Grondin, 2003, p.117). Utterly crushed by this personal slight, he began to doubt his own ability to do important philosophical work and reverted to more philologically oriented studies. Gadamer took a very long time to recover from this snub and remained philosophically inert for many years due to feelings of self-doubt. 'For a long time, writing tormented me', came a confession in later life, 'I always had the damned feeling that Heidegger was looking over my shoulder.' In fact he claims to have abandoned philosophy at this time in order to re-establish his connections with philology and classical thought and languages, a move away, that is, from the clutches of a harshly critical Martin Heidegger. Despite the rift, Heidegger agreed to supervise Gadamer's *Habilitation* thesis submitted in 1929 under the title, 'Interpretation of Plato's *Philebus'*. This is Gadamer's first substantial piece of philosophical work, published in 1931 under the title, *Plato's Dialectical Ethics*. During the war years Gadamer had little contact with Heidegger although after 1945 they re-established contact which lasted until Heidegger's death in 1976. Heidegger remains the most important figure in Gadamer's intellectual development and no other influence has had quite the same impact upon his mature philosophical work.

Both Gadamer and Heidegger remained in Germany during the Third Reich but whereas Heidegger shamefully fell under the influence of National Socialism (and this is well documented), Gadamer's relationship to the Nazis is much more sketchy and vague. Heidegger joined the Nazi Party in 1933 and as a consequence readily – albeit to the surprise of many of his students – took up the politically sensitive post of Rector at the University of Freiburg. His thought and writings during this year show evident signs of total acceptance of Nazi ideology. Although Heidegger was to sever links with the Nazi party shortly after this time, to his shame he never in later life apologized for his conduct during this period, nor did he publicly accept that he was guilty, to put it kindly, of a monstrous error of judgement.

Concerning Gadamer's conduct during the period of National Socialism, his own version is that he worked diligently throughout the war years on a small income. He had married Frida Katz in 1923 and in 1926 his first daughter Jutta was born. This marriage was to fall apart in the 1940s. Gadamer re-married in 1950. Life was hard during this period, as he had to make do with little more than a modest academic income, and to compound the misery hardship was widespread; this was the time of a financial crisis throughout Germany. He kept a low profile and accepted incremental academic advancement when it came his way. After the war, having avoided formal connection with the National Socialist Party, 'denazification' was unnecessary. This was not the case with Heidegger who was prevented from teaching for a number of years after the war. So untainted was Gadamer that the Russians supported his election to the position of Rector of the University of Leipzig (in what was to become East Germany) in the immediate post-war period of reconstruction. Leipzig was under Soviet domination in the initial post-war period and Gadamer moved west as soon as the opportunity arose, and when the professorship of Heidelberg, formerly Karl Jasper's position, fell vacant, he took up the position.

Throughout the war years there was little contact with Heidegger, but later a personal friendship was re-established lasting from the late 1940s, when Gadamer was Professor of Philosophy in Heidelberg, to the time of Heidegger's death in 1976. Heidegger's rehabilitation from post-war isolation was due in part to Gadamer although the popularization of his work by the post-war French thinkers, notably **Jean-Paul Sartre** and **Emmanuel Levinas** was equally important in Heidegger's being brought in from the cold. Gadamer organised the 1949 *Festschrift* for Heidegger's sixtieth birthday and was responsible for frequent invitations for Heidegger to lecture in Heidelberg. Unfortunately the master-pupil relationship endured, however, and Gadamer's awe in the presence of his former teacher clearly irked his own students who witnessed his continual subservience to Heidegger.

Although a full professor from a relatively early age he had not published a substantial work since his *Habilitation* thesis and throughout the 1950s he worked diligently but fitfully upon what was to become his *magnum opus*, **Truth and Method**. Gadamer's international reputation started after the publication in 1960 in Germany of **Truth and Method**. From this point onwards he rose from being a little-known commentator on Greek classical philosophy and well respected university teacher to one of the most important names in what came to be known as **philosophical hermeneutics**. The work was instantly recognized as an important work in Germany, and the debate it sparked off with the emerging young voice in social theory, Jürgen Habermas, added to its widening notoriety.

Gadamer retired from full-time university life in 1968 and at a time when most academics would be thinking of disengaging from professional activities and winding down scholarly commitments Gadamer's international career commenced. **Truth and Method** had put him on the global stage. He became a frequent visitor to the US for many years, notably Boston College, and travelled throughout the world attending conferences and introducing his brand of **philosophical hermeneutics** to a younger generation of academics. For all the emphasis in Gadamer's work upon tradition and a need to reclaim and retrieve the thoughts and ideas of the pre-modern world, Gadamer's work struck a chord with postmodern thinkers. His famous exchange in 1981 with **Jacques Derrida** in Paris, billed as a confrontation (or was it a showdown?) between hermeneutics and deconstruction, further enhanced Gadamer's reputation as an important thinker despite the fact that the meeting was something of a non-event, and hardly produced the fireworks, no doubt, many were expecting. Even in his later years Gadamer was still active writing papers and attending conferences and giving interviews, the usual trappings of celebrity and notoriety. As well as his more philosophical writings he took a keen interest in literature, especially the interpretation of lyric poetry, and his later reflections on contemporary German poets bear witness to this enthusiasm.

He died in 2002 at the biblically old age of 102. Even in very old age he remained mentally active and interested in world events. One of his last public statements came in an interview with the German newspaper *Die Welt* when he commented upon the 9/11 events saying, '*Es ist mir recht unheimlich geworden*' ('[the world] has become quite strange to me'. Quoted in Grondin, 2003, p. 335). This is one of Gadamer's few expressions of despair, as much of his later writing is on hope, not as a theological virtue but as a necessary secular feature of social life. The strangeness of the world Gadamer speaks of is, perhaps, a momentarily despairing comment upon his principal idea of hermeneutical conversation now rendered potentially obsolete and unworkable in the face of such world-dividing, dialogue-stopping incomprehensible events. At the heart of **philosophical hermeneutics** is the promise of something shared, a solidarity behind every disharmony. With 9/11 Gadamer possibly started to doubt this promise.

Despite the many works now available on Gadamer it is very difficult to get a full picture of the man; his likes and dislikes, his activities outside the academy, his character and personality. He was evidently a quiet and unassuming person yet urbane and gregarious, extremely generous with his time to students and by all accounts a forceful and charismatic teacher. A *bon viveur*, he liked good company, good conversation and good wine. He was clearly a cultured man, in the old-fashioned sense of cultured, being knowledgeable about high art, music and literature, especially modern German lyric poetry. Even in the modern world of installations, happenings and conceptual art, Gadamer evidently sought to make sense of these in his writings by showing that no matter how alienating and difficult artworks might appear there is always the possibility of dialogue. Artworks address us and we have a responsibility to listen.

As we have already noted, ***Truth and Method***, Gadamer's key work, was published when he was sixty. Prior to this time, although his list of published writings was quite short, he had worked since the 1930s on the philosophy of **Plato** and **Aristotle**. What was revolutionary about his mature work was his ability to use his nascent hermeneutics as a strategy for interpreting ancient texts. His writings on Plato and Aristotle are original, and he throws light on Plato by offering a hermeneutical account of the nature of dialogue and why Plato used dialogue rather than any other means of communicating his ideas. The standard view that Plato's work defends a universalist account of **truth** is challenged by Gadamer's stress upon the provisional, tentative and fallible nature of human knowledge and that the dialogue makes this position apparent. As well as this, Gadamer undermines the orthodox idea that Aristotle's work, in its mature phase, is a complete repudiation of Platonism. Gadamer succeeds in showing that **Aristotle** never moves far beyond Plato and the idea of a radical rupture between the two lacks hermeneutical plausibility, if anything there is a genuine unity between the two.

As a writer Gadamer's style is elegant and uncluttered. His subject matter may be difficult and his sheer range of erudition and scholarship may impress but his written style is very clear. ***Truth and Method*** presents the reader with a formidable challenge, if only because the work is so long and desultory, but the arguments are clearly stated and Gadamer's lifelong mission as an educator and pedagogue are evident via his desire to communicate. He seldom lapses into opacity and obscurity even though the structure of ***Truth and Method*** is at times a little shaky.

Curiously Gadamer wrote very little of substance before his groundbreaking ***Truth and Method*** in 1960. There are various reasons to account for this. 'Inner emigration', the strategy of many academics and intellectuals who did not leave Germany during the Third Reich but maintained a stubborn silence as a kind of passive resistance, is partial explanation for Gadamer's failure to produce more than a handful of papers during this period. And after the war Gadamer, in Leipzig as Rector, had a large administrative burden and this kept him away from publishing his research. A more compelling reason for Gadamer's modest output until he had almost reached retirement age was the emphasis he placed upon teaching. In the interview with Jonathan Rée and Christian Gehron for *Radical Philosophy*, when asked about whether writing was, for him, a pleasure, he makes the following revealing confession: 'No, it is violence. It is torture. Dialogue is fine. Even an interview! But writing for me is always an enormous self-torture. ... My main work was published when I was already sixty. My prestige as a teacher was quite high, and I had been a full professor for a long time. But I had not published much work. I invested more of my energy in teaching.'

The Gadamer-Derrida debate   (See **Derrida**.)

The Gadamer-Habermas debate   **Jürgen Habermas**, the philosopher and social theorist, wrote a lengthy review of Gadamer's *Truth and Method*. The review was largely sympathetic to the hermeneutical project but not uncritical and it sparked off a debate, in the form of an exchange of essays, between the two thinkers. Habermas takes issue with Gadamer's idea that his **philosophical hermeneutics** is universal in its application, that is, that all aspects of social life are fundamentally hermeneutical. Against this Habermas speaks of 'ideology-critique', a level of explanation that goes deeper than the hermeneutical, involving the social criticism of ideologies and the exposure of those ideological distortions which lack the kind of agreement Gadamer's hermeneutical understanding presupposes. The thought here, challenging Gadamer, is that human understanding is not a benign transaction as the hermeneutical **fusion of horizons** suggests. It is in fact a site where communication is 'systematically distorted', to use Habermas' phrase, by the largely unconsciously regulated social mechanisms of power and domination. Instead of hermeneutics Habermas recommends a 'universal pragmatics', an amalgamation of insights from psychoanalysis and ideology-critique, providing a context whereby communicative distortions are rooted out and genuine **dialogue** is then possible. Habermas is also unwilling to accept Gadamer's benign reading of tradition which he takes to be dogmatic and conservative. There is an alleged relativism in Gadamer's conception of **tradition** because it fails to provide a criterion for itself which is not self-referential; in other words, based on Gadamer's account there is no way of testing the epistemological credentials of tradition. Habermas sees Gadamer as a relativist because there is no ultimate court of appeal for the validity of tradition. Habermas needs some kind of transcendental principle to ground reason, rather than an account of rationality that is no more than a modality of tradition and **language**.

Habermas is a defender of the emancipatory and critical ideals of the **Enlightenment** and he takes his criticism further in claiming that Gadamer's account of tradition offers no possibility of critique. The claim is that Gadamer ignores the fact that within traditions there are often counter-traditions and traditions that subvert the main tradition. Gadamer's tradition is too conservative, too uncritical of the status quo. (See the **Derrida-Gadamer debate**.)

God Gadamer's religious position is best described as agnostic since he never denies the existence of God but leaves the matter of the reality of a deity an open question. Although he on occasions refers to himself as a Protestant and allies himself to the Lutheranism of his upbringing, he did not practise a religious faith. But Gadamer speaks, in his work, of the desire for transcendence although he never assumes this to be possible through religious faith and belief: the closest we come to transcendence, on Gadamer's account, is through art. His father, of a strongly scientific and positivistic bent, had little time for religion. On the other hand his mother affirmed a strong pietistic faith but this had little influence upon Gadamer as his mother died when he was in infancy. Although Gadamer never affirmed a strong religious faith he is always, in his work, deeply respectful of theology and religious experience. More than this he is aware of the strong debt his **philosophical hermeneutics** owes to the earlier theological hermeneutics of biblical interpretation. Critics have also pointed to the ways the explication of **philosophical hermeneutics** depends on a sympathetic reading of the theological writings of **Augustine**, **Aquinas** and the wider scholastic tradition. Other critics have suggested that Gadamer's work can be used for a hermeneutical defence of Christian theology in that in both cases there can be no last word on the matter of **understanding** (in general and on the nature of God in particular); it is always underway, incomplete and essentially incompletable. Gadamer's emphasis on our intimate connection with our cultural past also places him alongside those western churches that put great emphasis on the abiding influence and authority of **tradition**. Gadamer's most sustained published reflections upon religion took place on the isle of Capri and were part of a dialogue with the Italian philosopher **Gianni Vattimo** and the French philosopher **Jacques Derrida**.

—H—

Habermas, Jürgen (1929–)   Habermas is Germany's foremost living philosopher and social theorist. He was born in Düsseldorf and studied philosophy at the universities of Göttingen, Zürich and Bonn. As part of the second generation of critical theorists, he worked at the Institute for Social Research in Frankfurt as the assistant to **Theodor Adorno**. He subsequently took up professorial appointments in Heidelberg and Frankfurt. His work spans many academic disciplines and areas of concern. Marxism and the mainstream tradition of modern German philosophy, pragmatism and analytic philosophy have all influenced Habermas's social philosophy and seminal work on language. In recent years he has engaged in debates about postmodernism, Europe, bioethics, terrorism and religion. His works include: *The Theory of Communicative Action, Volume 1* (1981), *The Philosophical Discourse of Modernity* (1985), *Moral Consciousness and Communicative Action* (1983).

Habermas was one of the first to review Gadamer's *Truth and Method* and although he found much to commend in its general position he was quite critical. This sparked off an exchange of essays and articles which came to be known as the **Gadamer-Habermas** debate.

Health   (See *The Enigma of Health*.)

Hegel, Georg Wilhelm Friedrich (1770–1831)   Georg Wilhelm Friedrich Hegel was one of the most influential of the early nineteenth century German idealist philosophers. Born in Stuttgart in 1770, he studied theology in Tübingen. He worked as a private tutor and a schoolmaster for many years before taking up the professorship in philosophy in Heidelberg and then in the University of Berlin. He died in 1831 during a cholera epidemic. His principal works are *The Phenomenology of Spirit* (1807), *The Science of Logic* (1816) and *The Philosophy of Right* (1821). After his death many other works were published including, *Lectures on the Philosophy of History*, *Lectures on the Philosophy of Religion*, *Lectures on the History of Philosophy* and *Lectures on Aesthetics*. The cornerstone of Hegel's philosophy is the notion of *Geist* or 'Spirit'. Spirit is mind or ideas and because the universe is made up of nothing but ideas, Hegel's philosophy is a form of idealism. Spirit is not just human mind or intellectual activity;

it is what constitutes the whole of creation and is in a constant state of change and movement. What motivates this change? According to Hegel, the whole of history, natural as well as human, is a vast odyssey of Spirit in the process of coming to know and actualize itself through contradictions that are temporarily overcome and taken to a higher level: this is Hegel's **dialectic**. Ultimately, Spirit's journey will achieve some kind of resolution in what Hegel calls the Absolute, that point at which all the contradictions of history are overcome and resolved and Spirit comes to full recognition of itself. At the level of human history this means that all cultures are the embodiment of Spirit as it progresses to higher – that is more rational – forms of association. Central to Hegel's philosophy is the overcoming of one of the central problems in Western thought, the subject-object dichotomy. Because his idealism starts from the existence of Spirit there is no division between subjects and objects, or minds and matter. Although Hegel overcomes the scepticism which subject-object dualism gives rise to, the price he pays is enormous: all human activity is denied real agency, as everything becomes part of an inexorable sequence of historical devel-opment. Spirit is the driving force of all world history and this seems to deny the possibility of individual human agency.

What is the importance of Hegel to Gadamer's work? Gadamer has written a good deal about **Hegel**. There is an extended discussion of him in Part 3 of *Truth and Method* and a collection of essays on the notion of Hegelian **dialectic** (see *Hegel's Dialectic: Five Hermeneutical Studies*). Gadamer speaks of his relationship to Hegel as a 'tension-filled proximity'. By this he means that they share much in common but there is also much that divides them. What they share is a philosophical rejection of the subject-object division. Gadamer does not embrace the idea of Spirit (*Geist*) but in many ways his notion of **tradition** is quite Hegelian; to such an extent some might say, that he merely substitutes **tradition** for Spirit and uses it as a device for overcoming the traditional epistemological division between subjects and objects. The argument goes something like this. In Gadamer, genuine **dialogue** is made possible by the **fusion of horizons** and this in turn is made possible by the fact that the interpreter (subject) and the text (object), for example, are no more than aspects of a wider association, that is, **tradition**, and hence there is commonality and no alienation between the two. This is not unlike the subject and object relationship, which is ultimately an alternative description of what Hegel calls Spirit.

Another aspect of Gadamer's Hegelianism is his **historicism**. We spoke above of the odyssey of Spirit in the process of coming to know and actualize itself through contradictions that are provisionally overcome and taken to a higher level. This odyssey is no less than the course of world history. The basis of Hegel's vision is Spirit's development. This development is teleological, meaning that Spirit is moving towards its goal in the same way as an acorn becomes an oak tree. Spirit's full actualization is when it comes to an end point of history; Hegel calls this the Absolute. Although Gadamer tells a similar story about the unfolding of **tradition** through history, he denies it any kind of teleological status, for there is no *terminus ad quem* for historical development, and no Absolute where all the contradictions of history are resolved. For Gadamer, there is incessant historical change but this is not structured teleologically.

Hegel's Dialectic: Five Hermeneutical Studies* (1971)**   Gadamer's treatise on the Hegelian dialectic represents a seminal text in the development of his **philosophical hermeneutics** in which the theory of interpretation advanced in ***Truth and Method is applied to an exposition of a theorist who continuously influenced Gadamer's work. As such, Gadamer's examination of Hegel does not resign itself to a mere summary of the Hegelian dialectic, but rather, in accordance with his theory of historically effective consciousness, elucidates what in Hegel resounds in the present theoretical horizon. Since the dialectic as developed by Hegel remained immanent to Gadamer's conception of hermeneutics, the essays in this work, as well as contributing to a concise exegesis on the former's system, also elucidate the productive tension between the two theories. For Gadamer, the subject-object dialectic, as presented in *The Phenomenology of Spirit* and further refined in *The Science of Logic*, can be conceived as a modern apotheosis of the self-movement of thought that for him characterized the dialectics of the ancients and to which he constantly returns in the elaboration of his own hermeneutics. Gadamer's dialogical conception of hermeneutics is thus informed through an idiosyncratic synthesis of the Platonic and Hegelian dialectical method, and accordingly the development of this appropriation can be discerned throughout the work. The recurrence of the Platonic principle of the self-progression of thought within the Hegelian system is made explicit by Gadamer in the initial chapter of the book in which he argues that the speculative elements of the dialectic, existing within the fluidity of concepts, is analogous to the radical dynamics of language. However, indication of the influence of Hegel's dialectic on Gadamer's own thought is not limited to a comparison with Plato; rather it can be discerned within the uniqueness of his interpretation of some of the central passages from Hegel's work. In his analysis of 'Dialectic of Self-Consciousness', Gadamer presents us with a perspicacious examination of the development of consciousness of the self that seeks to alter the influential interpretation by the Hegel scholar Alexandre Kojève. According to Gadamer, the thesis of the reversal of the dependency between master and servant is insufficient to capture the full extent of what Hegel presents us with. Although accurate to an extent, such an interpretation relies on an external limitation imposed on the master and leaves unconsidered the dialectical reversal *within* the consciousness of the master. For Gadamer this dialectical reversal constitutes the awareness of the inferiority of the master, of its inability to recognise its being-for-self as truth. As for Hegel, the absolute master is represented within the ineluctable universality of death. Pure being-for-self exists for Gadamer in the recognition of finitude, in the authentic comportment towards death. Gadamer here presents us with an image of Hegel as prescient of the fundamental concerns of later theorists including Heidegger whose thesis on the 'forgetfulness of being' was already anticipated in Hegel's dialectic. Although Gadamer fundamentally disagrees with the teleology of the Hegelian dialectic, instead finding its true vindication within the fluidity of language, the analysis of Hegel presented throughout the work demonstrates the necessity of his **dialectic** and as such develops a number of Gadamer's core theses initially formulated in *Truth and Method*.

Heidegger, Martin, (1889–1976)   One of the most original thinkers of the twentieth century, a student of **Edmund Husserl**, and the teacher of Gadamer. The phenomenology of Edmund Husserl offered Heidegger a means of escaping the perceived historical relativism of Dilthey's philosophy and gave hermeneutics, now perceived as a phenomenological hermeneutics, a solid footing, transforming it into an ontology of existence. In the first part of *Being and Time* (1927), Heidegger takes up the concept of 'phenomenon', which indicates the manner in which something shows itself from itself. That is, not what is simply visible, but what shows or offers itself, its manifesting light. However, according to Heidegger, the appearance of what shows itself is also an announcement of self-concealing in which concealing appears along with the uncovering. From this, Heidegger argues that truth and un-truth belong together, and the manifestation of being necessarily goes together with a form of concealment. In a word, the finitude of the manifestation of being corresponds to the finitude of human *Dasein*. Heidegger's thought thus lays the foundation for a notion of truth as 'disclosure' (*a-létheia*), i.e. existential disclosive understanding, and not simply as *adaequatio*, which is the basis of his original hermeneutic phenomenology. Since the phenomenon that shows itself belongs to the truth of the *logos* as understanding, 'correspondence' and 'adequation' are seen as derivative phenomena, i.e. the logical content of valid propositions are themselves founded upon existential-ontological understanding which is affectively attuned or disposed to its world. It follows that if truth is rooted in our way of attuned being-in-the-world and the *logos* is primarily a way of uncovering, a letting something be seen, then *lógos apophantikos*, traditionally understood as the *locus classicus* of truth, can no longer be considered the primary site of truth. Hence, both realism and idealism – the two antithetical conceptions of the relationship between the *lógos* and being, positions which have characterized Western philosophy hitherto – fail to get to grips with truth in its original sense as the event of a truth process.

Heidegger takes from **Husserl** the notion of language as containing a signifying power, according to which the sign is not simply a relation that refers to a designated object, but contains within itself something of the thing designated. According to this phenomenological perspective, language is not exhausted in pointing beyond itself, insofar as it shows or uncovers the ontological structure of reference itself. As Husserl had it, the life-world is the basis not only of eidetic intuition, but also of language, that lived dimension which underpins existential and pre-categorial concepts and words, and makes up the human community as essentially a linguistic community. This is so because the life-world is the horizon of the pre-understanding of our ideas and words, and language always refers to something beyond itself, a field of associations, relationships and existential implications, towards the horizon of the world as the horizon of meaning, understanding and interpretation.

In a very original way, Heidegger's hermeneutics offers an immanent critique of Husserl's notion of phenomenological reflection and intuition and assigns a specific and unique task to lived understanding and interpretation, defining his thought as existential and ontological hermeneutics, i.e. an analytic of existential comportment, or a phenomenology of existential, attuned understanding. *Dasein*, not constituting consciousness and its intentional acts, as the structure of human existence, is understood as an openness to and concern for the meaning of being, i.e. the conditions of its actual comprehension. The hermeneutics of *Being and Time* is above all an eidetic analysis of existence and its fundamental ontological structures that trace the horizon of its disclosive being open, grasped as discursive understanding and interpretation. Since the whole process of under-standing and interpretation takes place in language, it therefore articulates what is linguistically understandable. Language is thus a manifestation of the existential and historical structures of mankind, the historical form or structure underwriting human existence and the meaning of being.

Heidegger's hermeneutics therefore mindfully enacts the very mode of our understanding of reality and is conditioned by the manner of its disclosure. Hermeneutics is interpretation because it is the uncovering of being through discursive understanding. It stands behind every methodology or interpre-tative technique because this method is a way of getting to the appearance of being, in all its ways of being, insofar as being is not a thing, but rather the event of a thing's coming into being. However, Heidegger's later thought addresses the paths of language according to the paths of the poets, neither of which are reducible to logic and reason, and hermeneutics is no longer conceived as an art of interpretation or an analytic of existence, but rather as a listening to language, i.e. correspondence between being and its truth.

Heidegger's influence upon Gadamer is profound, protracted and his work could be read, with qualifications, as a homage to his teacher. The young Gadamer learned almost everything from Heidegger's various ways of thinking and interpreting the Greeks, and it was Heidegger's early lectures on Aristotle that ignited Gadamer's imagination. As he put it: hearing Heidegger was like 'an electric shock', and it was Heidegger's emphasis upon 'historical situatedness', 'finitude', 'facticity' and 'projective understanding' that drew Gadamer into a lifelong conversation with his teacher. However, it would be wrong to suggest that Gadamer merely appropriated or passively inherited a set of philosophical questions from Heidegger. He did more than that, and his own brand of philosophical hermeneutics, contrary to **Habermas'** reading, is in no way reducible to the mere 'urbanization of the Heideggerian Province'. While Gadamer did not write anything about Heidegger until 1960, his conversations with Heidegger, and the impact his teacher's rigorous and radical questioning had upon him, drove him to question the very presuppositions which underpin Heidegger's philosophy and forced him to respond to and independently challenge the philosophical implications of his teacher's original path of thinking. In order for Gadamer to find his own voice, i.e. to find his own independent and unique style of thinking, he turned to the Greeks and attempted to re-read **Plato** and **Aristotle** anew. What this means is that Gadamer's interpretation of the Greeks, an interpretation which deviates from Heidegger's own readings of antiquity, could be read as his attempt to put light between himself and Heidegger's original, albeit somewhat seductive and agenda-laden, readings of the tradition.

There are many different points of divergence and similarity but let me highlight one specific difference: Gadamer's criticism of the 'other' in Heidegger's thought. In a late essay on 'Subjectivity and Intersubjectivity', Gadamer highlights his unease with Heidegger's analysis of the other in his existential-ontology. While Gadamer believes that Heidegger's existential-ontological approach makes radical inroads, surpassing Husserl's transcendental approach to subjectivity and intersubjectivity, he nonetheless claims that the other can only appear or show itself in Heidegger's thought as a limiting factor, while for Gadamer the more pressing question is: Why is it that I can only experience and understand my own limitations anew through a dialogical encounter with the other? He writes:

> 'I was trying, in opposition to Heidegger, to show how the understanding of the Other possesses a fundamental significance. ... In the end, I thought the very strengthening of the Other against myself would, for the first time, allow me to open up the real possibility of understanding. To allow the Other to be valid against Oneself – and from there to let all my hermeneutic works slowly develop – is not only to recognize in principle the limitation of one's own framework, but is also to allow one to go beyond one's own possibilities, precisely in a dialogical, communicative, hermeneutic process' ('Subjectivity and Intersubjectivity', p. 284).

What Gadamer is after in his response to Heidegger is the possibility of surpassing or transcending one's enclosed self-understanding via the other as a hermeneutic and dialogical partner.

Underlining his devotion to Plato and Aristotle, it is the good will inherent in Gadamer's notion of keeping oneself open to the ambiguous alterity at

play in every human conversation, of being the open-minded *phronimos* when engaging in conversation, which becomes the framework for his critical, albeit often implicit, appropriation of Heidegger's phenomeno-logical hermeneutics. However, Gadamer's own philosophy is more of a nuanced debate with Heidegger than an all out critique, and it is his notion of **effective-historical consciousness**, and later **linguisticality**, which delimits this debate. Of course, Heidegger's presentation of the surrounding structure of history, within which existential historicality and understanding are thought, is precisely what Heidegger applied to historicality itself. Gadamer's notion of **effective-historical consciousness**, in which Hegel's speculative dialectics and Heidegger's concept of projection on the basis of thrownness are brought together, was his attempt to orient thinking to the concrete and effective reality of historical tradition, which is expressed most fully in the participatory life of conversation and finite reflection. This linguistic life of conversation and reflection is best defined as the enactment of a historically situated understanding which is never fully transparent to itself.

Heidegger's Ways (1983) In this collection of fifteen essays, lectures and speeches, Gadamer presents his account of the thought of **Heidegger**. This collection is important for Gadamer studies because it gives valuable insights into what he took from Heidegger's work and also, importantly, what he rejected. For example, in the 1968 essay 'The language of metaphysics', Gadamer rejects Heidegger's verdict that language, especially technical language, has become thoroughly tainted by metaphysics. (See **Heidegger**.)

Heraclitus (540–475 BCE) Pre-socratic Greek philosopher best known for his obscure epigrams. He denied the existence of being and asserted that all was becoming, i.e. existence is, like fire, unstable, and in a constant state of change and transformation. Gadamer connects the fragments of Heraclitus to the development of Greek philosophy and science in *The Beginning of Knowledge* and other essays.

Hermeneutics of suspicion The 'masters of suspicion', as identified by the French hermeneutical philosopher **Paul Ricoeur**, are **Friedrich Nietzsche**, Karl Marx and **Sigmund Freud**. All three thinkers have taught us that there are hidden meanings behind the obvious ones or meanings that are consistent with, or opposed to, those intended by the author. For Nietzsche, lurking behind everything is 'will to power' so we should not take on trust what a person says; we should dig down to a deeper level to expose the desire for power which betrays the real meaning of a text. Karl Marx does not read texts innocently. From his perspective all texts must be read as betraying the writer's class position, his or her relation to the means of production. So, for example, to gain access to the real meaning of a novel we should read it suspiciously as a defence or at least a manifestation of the outlook of a particular social class. **Sigmund Freud** completes the triumvirate. The hermeneutic of suspicion here is to ignore what a person says and seek to uncover the traces of the Unconscious, hence texts are read suspiciously as evidence of fantasy and unconscious wish-fulfilment and other manifestations of instinctual drives.

Gadamer has been accused of naivety about the hermeneutic of suspicion being oblivious to the dimensions of meaning that run against the force field of intended meanings. Ideology-critique, a term popularised by **Habermas**, seeks to expose the structures of capitalist domination and power that deform everyday communication. Such a critique is an evident form of the hermeneutic of suspicion and it is pitted against Gadamer's hermeneutics. (See the **Gadamer-Habermas debate**.)

Hermeneutics of trust (see also **Hermeneutics of suspicion**) Gadamer frequently speaks of the importance of trust, not just in relation to the interpretation of texts but in everyday life. Trust is important because we must assume that the text or person we engage with makes sense and that if there is ambiguity and something is readily misinterpreted we should give it the benefit of the doubt. In everyday conversation, as much as in everyday life, it is very easy, if you put your mind to it, wilfully to misunderstand what is said. This is true, but a hermeneutics of trust always works towards understanding rather than away from it. A hermeneutics of trust, very like the **principle of charity**, is usually contrasted with the **hermeneutics of suspicion**.

The Hermeneutic Circle It was **Friedrich Schleiermacher** who first sketched the limits of hermeneutics, understood simply as a philological method, and put forward the general problem of the circular structure of interpretation, insofar as he was trying to develop a general hermeneutics based not only on technical or philological grounds, but also on linguistic and philosophical ones. Schleiermacher's position was the first formulation of a philosophically oriented hermeneutics, understood as a reflection on the meaning of human understanding through language, and the centrality of the hermeneutic circle to this understanding. For Schleiermacher, the hermeneutic circle indicates the circular movement operative in textual interpretation, be it literary, philosophical or religious, a circle that binds the understanding of the entire text to an understanding of its parts.

Heidegger subsequently analysed this concept of the hermeneutic circle before it was taken up and developed by Gadamer, the latter emphasizing the circularity of the interpretative processes with particular reference to historical textuality. Given a text to interpret, this concept shows how the approach of the interpreter must be characterized by an unavoidable pre-given horizon of understanding which emanates from the text or from the historical and cultural context in which the author engages with it. As such, interpretative knowledge is a continuous interchange between concepts to be learned and concepts already learned or familiar, between learning and responding via the interpretative attitude. Knowledge is thus necessarily situated within a specific historical and psychological horizon and is the result of a stratification of circular concepts.

Building on Heidegger's insights, Gadamer claims that the interpreter can be accessed only through the interpretation of a series of pre-understandings or pre-judgments. Far from being a *tabula rasa*, the mind of the interpreter is replete with a set of expectations or models of meaning, or a multiplicity of provisional guidelines, which together constitute the preliminary hypothesis in the interpretation of various texts. This circle is known as a hermeneutic circle. Heidegger would have us understand how the problem hinges upon entering into the circle at the right point, and of avoiding a vicious circular movement by rendering thematic the situated prejudices or preconceptions that inhabit all interpretation. The aim here is to throw the interpreter back on his/her own initial preconceptions and to force the reader to come back to them, to review and correct them, through repeated comparison with the object or matter of interpretation. The hermeneutic circle does not involve closing the interpreter in upon themselves, but rather a systematic openness to the otherness of the text and to the voice of the other. Those who want to understand a text must be ready to say something to it and to let it speak its truth. Hence, interpretative consciousness must first be educated hermeneutically and sensitive to the slippages of the text.

As mentioned above, the notion of the hermeneutic circle is grounded, for Gadamer at least, in one of the most characteristic doctrines of his thought, namely the rehabilitation of prejudice, authority and tradition. Gadamer explains how prejudices are not something necessarily false, insofar as false or illegitimate prejudices are often accompanied by real or legitimate ones. Taken in isolation, then, prejudice simply means an opinion that is pronounced prior to a complete examination. In a word, Gadamer shows his readers how the circularity of prejudices are part and parcel of our social and historical reality.

Hermeneutics The etymology of the word 'hermeneutics' displays a confluence of meanings that have their origin in the different conceptions of hermeneutics itself. The term comes from the Greek word *hermeneía* (from the verb *hermeneúein*, which means to interpret or translate), subsequently corresponding to the Latin *interpretari*, and is the root of other derived words such as *hermeneús*, *hermeneutés*, *hermeneutiké*. Scholars have confirmed the intimate connection between the words 'hermeneutics', 'word' and 'language' in relation not only to the Latin word *verbum*, or *Wort* in German, but also emphasizing the difference between the traditional meaning of *hermeneía*, which indicates any activity of interpretation. More generally, the term is thought to have taken on a variety of senses, from the art of rhetoric as an unspoken thought being drawn out of darkness and into the clarity of linguistic expression; translation from one language to another; commentary; an explanation of the difficulties of meaning and interpretation of texts, be they religious or legal. The notion of hermeneutics developed in contemporary philosophy, which embraces not only the problems concerning the interpretation of texts – literary, philosophical or religious – but also the careful consideration of both the cultural and historical conditions that form the horizon of the text, constitutes the interpreter's horizon of 'pre-understanding'. The complex branching out of the term 'hermeneutics' stems from the interconnection of all these meanings that cover the technical (philological, linguistic or exegetical) interpretation of texts.

The origin of the meaning of hermeneutics is also connected to hermeneúos, a noun that can be related to the Greek god Hermes. Hermes was the messenger of the gods and bears the message of destiny as a guide in the underworld. The reference to Hermes, and to his nature as a messenger of the gods, is connected to Plato's use of intermediary figures that have the power to mediate and interpret. For example, in Plato's *Symposium* Eros interprets 'between gods and men, conveying and taking across to the gods the prayers and sacrifices of men, and to men the commands and replies of the gods; he is the mediator who spans the chasm which divides them, and therefore in him all is bound together' (*Symposium*, 202d).

For instance, with the etymological connection between Hermes and hermeneutics, Heidegger emphasizes that hermeneutics is a listening to the hidden or submerged meanings in language, and goes beyond the necessary analysis of the conditions of human understanding: it is these meanings that carry the message of the word and call for a reception and interpretation of the message. The myth of Hermes thus symbolizes any mediated communication: first, the mediator between gods and men, but also the mediation of men's thoughts in speech and writing, mediation between silence and speech and, even more deeply, mediation between falsehood and truth, between darkness and light, between the hidden and the manifest. But whatever the real tie that etymologically binds herme- neutics to Hermes, its symbolic language helps us to understand a range of meanings operative in contemporary hermeneutics that would otherwise be lost, particularly those relating to language as a listening to the word. The traditional notion of hermeneutics, by limiting itself to the field of pure textual exegesis, had in fact become a technical interpretation, i.e. a philological exegesis, forgetting that interpretation is primarily an existential process of drawing forth the truth through listening and not just a formal methodology for deciphering the meanings and meaning constellation of words.

With regard to its historical origins, these must be sought in the long process that for many reasons led early nineteenth-century scholars to the recognition of the autonomy of hermeneutics in the context of philosophy. Scholars emphasize a dual historical origin: on one hand, the origin is to be found in the reflections surrounding the understanding of Greek and the expression of truth by means of the *logos*, and on the other, in the inter- pretation of Sacred Scripture in the Judeo-Christian tradition. In particular, contemporary hermeneutics often develops and responds to principles and issues that originally arose in the context of interpreting sacred texts and the historical transmission of their understanding. Indeed, the main concepts of today's philosophical hermeneutics – the hermeneutic circle, the existential dimension of historical understanding, tradition, the primacy of the unsaid, application, the dialogical dimension of the experience of truth – are all issues that have their origin in the many ways in which hermeneutics was configured historically in its relationship with the word of scripture.

Alternatively, in the so-called Socratic dialogues, Plato presents through the figure of Socrates one of the most important examples of the hermeneut and this is most evident in the essential role that question and answer plays in the dialogue. Socrates shows that knowing how to ask the right question is key to knowing how to interpret and understand the nature of the problem under discussion. In the Socratic conception of question and answer, the answer is already contained in the questions you want answered, and when it comes to getting to the heart of the issue, it is a matter of a proper recollective retrieval of what one already knows. The very process of questioning is utilized in order to bring the listener towards the truth, and to allow it to be enacted and shared by the other in dialogue. For this reason, Gadamer argues that the hermeneutic experience implies the primacy of dialogue and the structure of question and answer.

The conception of the primacy of questioning has its roots in Gadamer's reading of Plato, even in the interpretation of texts that display the most modern version of hermeneutics. For instance, as is shown in Plato's *Phaedrus*, in the primacy of the spoken word over the written, the written text must somehow become oral speech, connecting it with a living conversation (see *Phaedrus*, 275–276b). Hence the text is not only an inert reality, receiving questions from the reader, but also a living reality that raises and poses questions of its own. So hermeneutical interpretation of the text means an ability to listen to the text, to pose questions to the text and to have questions posed to you from it.

It is with the figure of Socrates that Plato attempts to reanimate the dramatic contrast between *sophia*, philosophical or scientific knowledge divorced from the daily lives of men, and *phronesis* as a practical knowledge that leads to an insight which is fundamentally important to human life. The philosopher's search for the essence of man, what man is and what man ought to be, needs to be led by practical wisdom that can look after the interests of one's soul and its destiny. Knowledge that is purely formal and abstract, the metaphysical type, is not enough for the good life, to which only an ethics of *phronesis* allows access. Hence, philosophy takes its name not simply from *sophia*, but rather from the situated longing or yearning for it.

Plato develops a tension that is subsequently accentuated in contemporary hermeneutics: interpretation as a technique or an understanding of truth. The contemporary use of the term 'hermeneutics' supplements the Platonic conviction that saw in it an indication of a purely technical interpretation or translation, which is unable to grasp the truth. According to the later Heidegger and Gadamer, Plato strongly emphasizes the difference between hermeneutics understood as a technical device and a philosophy of interpretation and understanding that is basically an assent to the truth already nascent in the word. Plato also deals with the fundamental issue that truth cannot exist without being connected to the whole: only the dialectical and critical examination of different viewpoints makes it clear which path is the path to truth, and this path is the goal of Gadamer's philosophical and dialectical hermeneutics.

Aristotle's *On Interpretation* (*Peri Hermeneías*) offers another account of the first formulations of the problem of hermeneutic interpretation in the context of a philosophy of *logos* and being. According to the books of the *Organon*, *On Interpretation* contains the main arguments regarding the nature of a 'proposition' or 'judgment', i.e. *lógos apophantikós* as an expression in which there is either truth or falsity. Therefore an expression or a statement contains truth or falsity in the sense that, according to Aristotelian logic, nouns and verbs, when taken separately, are neither true nor false, but may indicate the true or the false once they are combined in a logical proposition. Therefore, according to Aristotle, not all propositions contain truth or falsity, but only the propositions that express a judgment about the truth, and then connect the words in order to express meaning in making a deliberate reference to reality. Thus the basic words that make up a sentence contain neither truth nor falsity, and so are outside the problem of hermeneutics, which is concerned with propositions that are both linguistic expressions and logical expressions of judgment.

Unlike Plato, Aristotle's hermeneutics is also a hermeneutics of the proposition and not of speech and language in general, which is in contrast with the hermeneutic conception of language as a totality that gives meaning to individual words and sentences. On the other hand, a logical proposition is for Aristotle an expression of an intellectual act. Hence the primacy of language as the horizon for understanding truth, thematized by hermeneutic philosophy, has lead to a reversal of the traditionally accepted Aristotelian thesis regarding the primacy of logical judgment and its essential relation to truth.

However, it is somewhat simplistic to reduce Aristotle to the context of an analytic study of grammatical-linguistic propositions. Aristotle also made a significant contribution to a hermeneutics of truth that begins with the important distinction between the 'expressed word' and the 'inner word', which highlights the distinction between 'saying' and 'expressing'. Secondly, Aristotle's *Peri Hermeneias* established for the first time that in any meaningful discourse, regardless of its nature, it is impossible to separate the 'use' we make of words from the grammatical structures that support this use, which ultimately support the logical structures of thought. Grammar and logic make the use of words understandable in language that would otherwise remain only words for things or concepts. In addition and following on from Plato's discussion in the soul's dialogue with itself, the soul's participation in dialogue, in the *Phaedrus*, Aristotle's 'hermeneutics' states that interpretation is discourse itself and 'the sounds articulated by the voice are symbols of states of the soul, and written words are symbols of words uttered in speech' (*On Interpretation*, §I). Thus for Aristotle the spoken word is a symbol or a sign of affections of the soul; written words are the signs of spoken words.

Taking Heidegger's phenomenological hermeneutics and his early reading of Aristotle's *Nicomachean Ethics, Physics and Rhetoric* as the foundation for a reflection on the meaning of human understanding, Gadamer argues that understanding is not only an existential event, but also a historical, linguistic and dialectical event. Gadamer's **philosophical hermeneutics** is thus characterized by a dialectical and dynamic movement which is not simply analytic and descriptive, insofar as it develops an understanding of Heidegger's ontological hermeneutics, but rehabilitates the dialectical or dialogical aspect of philosophy that Heidegger wanted to overcome by means of an immanent critique. This important dialectical element, which is demonstrated in his book *Plato's Dialectical Ethics* from 1931, acquires the character of experience and **fusion of horizons**, and this dialectical and dialogical movement are imported into and fused with the structures of existential understanding developed by Heidegger.

The relationship between 'historical existence' and 'hermeneutic under-standing' is assessed by Gadamer based on a prior understanding which is not only existential but is instead grounded in preconceptual knowledge which guides our concrete historical existence. More importantly, this preconceptual knowledge cannot be jettisoned for the sake of conceptual purity and complete rational determination. Beyond and perhaps challenging Heidegger, Gadamer explores the question of 'historical consciousness' as consciousness not only of the conditions of existential understanding, but of all the factors and components involved in our 'historical understanding', factors which establish the relationship between our present and our historical past.

Unlike Heidegger, Gadamer succeeds in asserting that our prior under-standing is not only existential or ontological, but that it is fully inserted into a tradition that constitutes the true historical horizon of our conscious being in the world. Our prejudices are not something abstract or purely ontological but are products of a history which is precisely the **tradition**. And it is for this reason that we must engage the historical **tradition**, which does not simply mean appealing to the past as the source of our subjectivity, but rather recognizing in history those elements of **tradition** which are present and which make themselves felt.

The **hermeneutic circle** becomes, then, for Gadamer, a movement that leads the interpreter to gather together the entire tradition of under-standing, textual and non-textual, going via the individual partners in the historical tradition of its interpretation, searching with fidelity, looking for a unity of meaning in the text and recognizing the similarities between the different traditions of understanding. The hermeneutic circle is based essentially on the inextricable relationship of language, understanding, history and the life-world. This is so because every understanding of reality is linguistically mediated and language is always conditioned by its historical and existential pre-understanding. Thus, every historical understanding, be it aesthetic, cultural or philosophical, is subject to historical belonging, or to a cultural tradition and the language that forms the horizon of understanding.

Gadamer's **philosophical hermeneutics** is therefore concerned with knowledge of the history of effects or **effective historical consciousness** (*wirkungsgeschichtliche Bewußtsein*), which means that the consciousness operative in hermeneutic understanding is rooted within historical understanding as an understanding of the effects engendered by the history of textual interpretations. There are two fundamental concepts which form the backbone of Gadamer's hermeneutics: 1) the interpretative reception of texts throughout history is determined by the particular existential, cultural and religious concerns that the reader who reads the text is experiencing; and 2) from this is derived the concept of interpretation as application within a given socio-cultural or historico-existential context. This is the privileged moment that Gadamer calls '**fusion of horizons**', by means of which the interpreter, overcoming the temporal distance that separates him/her from a text and its author, starts actually to broaden his/her own interpretative horizon, allowing the assumptions of the past to be the necessary elements that enrich his/her understanding.

Hirsch, Eric Donald (1928–)   American literary critic and educationalist, best known for his controversial idea of 'cultural literacy', i.e. the idea of a body of knowledge requisite for responsible citizenship. His early work, *Validity in Interpretation* (1967), contained one of the first English language reviews of **Truth and Method**. Defending a traditional account of meaning as the reproduction of the author's intended meaning, Hirsch is strongly critical of Gadamer's notion of the **fusion of horizons**. If the meaning of a text, for example, is a fusing of the author's semantic intentions and those of the interpreter, then textual meaning is nihilistic and open to radical indeterminacy where meaning is unstable. Hence for Hirsch **philosophical hermeneutics** is guilty of linguistic relativism, that is, the destruction of fixed meanings. On this account Gadamer can be likened to Lewis Carroll's Humpty Dumpty who claims, 'when I use a word ... it means just what I choose it to mean!' For Hirsch, Gadamer fails to observe a central distinction between meaning and significance. The difference, for Hirsch, is this: meaning is fixed and immutable whereas significance is ephemeral and determined by historical, and, in his eyes, purely subjective judgements. But whereas meaning should take precedence over significance, the distinction in Gadamer's work is blurred, as the two are interchangeable.

Historical consciousness   Consciousness, for Gadamer, is never an individual ego or subject reflecting in a void, after the fashion of **René Descartes** and his cogito argument. It is invariably historical in the sense that consciousness happens within a context where the specific cultural past of **tradition** constantly operates. (See **historically effected consciousness**.)

Historical distance   This refers to an apparent gap or distance between the interpreter in the present and a text or event in the past. Part of the problem of interpretation is to overcome the alienating historical distance between past and present. According to **philosophical hermeneutics** the distance is in fact illusory for both past and present are part of a continuum, which is **tradition**. The interpreter in the present is actually at no distance from the past because, through **tradition**, the past is always working with the present. (See **historically effected consciousness**.)

'Historically effected consciousness'   (also referred to as **'effective historical consciousness'**) Gadamer refers to 'effective history' meaning the history of effects: 'understanding is, essentially, a historically effected event' (**TM**, p. 300). This is a difficult thought to grasp. What Gadamer has in mind is that the position of the interpreter, or the one who seeks to understand, is not fixed (as science conceives its detached observer to be); on the contrary, the interpreter is always, as part of tradition, the effect of prior interpretation. There can be no neutral position from which interrogation or understanding takes place as the site of interpretation is itself the effect of the past upon the present. The sovereignty of the subject is once again taken to be fictional since the interpreter is little more than the effect of tradition rather than its controlling subject. What then is one conscious of in 'effective historical consciousness'? We are conscious of the tradition and the way it has its effect. The prejudices of the individual can never be raised to the level of consciousness. Because the **prejudices** are themselves the condition of consciousness, they can never be raised to the level of reflective judgement. But the effect of the disruption of the prejudices can be experienced, i.e. felt as an effect. Once again, the model of textual interpretation will provide the clue to unravelling the identity between understanding and interpretation. When reading a text it is understood not simply by making sense of the words on the page but by permitting the horizon of the text to fuse with the horizon of the reader in such a way that the reader is affected by the encounter with the text. It is a common enough experience to be disrupted by the effect a text can have on the reader; often what we take for granted can be redefined, changed and realigned by the act of reading. Gadamer speaks here of consciousness. A consciousness in the act of reading is never fully present to itself but it can be made aware of changes taking place (in that consciousness) as the text has an effect. In its capacity to surprise, delight, intrigue, confuse and so on, we can speak of the effect the text has upon consciousness. Gadamer seeks to dispel the orthodox idea that consciousness is reflection fully in control of itself: he conceives of consciousness as both active and re-active.

The idea of an effect is important in another way. Not only is the reader an effect of the text, as the horizons of reader and text fuse; the reader is also revealed to be part of an historical effect: 'Every encounter with tradition that takes place within historical consciousness involves the experience of a tension between the text and the present' (*TM*, p. 306).

There is a constant dialogue at work in interpretation, a dialogue between the past and the present. The past does not have to be the distant past of antiquity – it can be the recent past of a moment just gone; the point is that in both cases the same hermeneutical problem arises: how can the interpreter in the present accommodate or negotiate meanings external to current consciousness? Gadamer's whole point is that there are no meanings external to current consciousness, since meaning itself is always produced by the coming together of the immediate and the point of tradition one seeks to understand.

Historicism   According to the Austrian philosopher **Karl Popper**, historicism is the belief that there are irons laws of history and once these laws have been discovered it is possible to predict the future on the basis of the past. Popper was right to show that there is a version of historicism that is more like prophecy, evoking pseudo-scientific causal laws for explaining the present and predicting the future. He neglected to disclose that there is a more benign sense of historicism – the one sustaining the tradition from **Hegel** to **Dilthey** to **Heidegger** and beyond; the one that affirms **historicity**, the essentially historical nature of all understanding. In this more positive sense it is quite appropriate to describe Gadamer's work as historicist.

Historicity/historicality   Accepting that the foundation of Heidegger's phenomenological hermeneutics is tied to a reflection on the meaning of human understanding, Gadamer believes that understanding is not only an existential-ontological event but also a historical, linguistic and dialectical event. Gadamer's **philosophical hermeneutics** is hence characterized by a historically dynamic structure insofar as it develops an understanding of Heidegger's ontological hermeneutics that he calls dialectical or dialogical. The dialectical element is present in order to capture the essence of genuine experience, first analyzed in the Platonic dialogues, and to bring it together with Heidegger's existential ontological understanding of being in a way that does not still the dynamics of experience into a simple static method.

The relationship between 'historical existence' and 'hermeneutic understanding' is determined by Gadamer based on a pre-understanding which is not only existential but, on the basis of 'pre-concepts' of knowledge, related to concrete historical existence, which cannot be accessed by means of a purely conceptual leap. Even more than Heidegger, Gadamer explores the question of 'historical consciousness' as consciousness not only of the conditions of existential understanding, but of all those factors and components impacting in a decisive way on our historical understanding, and establishing a relationship between the living present and the historical past.

Unlike Heidegger, and drawing heavily on Hegel, Gadamer asserts that our pre-understanding is not only existential or ontological, but that it is fully inserted into a traditional culture of **historical consciousness**, which constitutes the true historical horizon of human experience. Our prejudices are not purely ontological, but are produced by a history that is precisely embedded in tradition. Engaging the historical tradition is not about appealing to the past from which our subjectivity springs, but recognizing in history precisely those elements of tradition that are operatively present and which have been handed down to us. In short, Gadamer's understanding of experience and historicity is fused insofar as genuine experience for Gadamer is an experience of one's own historicity as an experience of finitude. However, Gadamer is quick to add that one's historicity is deeply bound up with one's relationship to the other, writing:

> 'The genuine meaning of our finitude or our thrownness
> consists in the fact that we become aware not only of our
> being historically conditioned, but especially of our being

conditioned by the other. Precisely in our ethical relation to
the other, it becomes clear to us how difficult it is to do justice
to the demands of the other or even simply to become aware
of them. The only way not to succumb to our finitude is to
open ourselves to the other, to listen to the 'thou' who stands
before us' (*A Century in Philosophy*, p. 29).

History of philosophy   Gadamer's work is a constant engagement
with the principal ideas and figures in the history of Western philosophy.
Truth and Method and later works make constant references to classical
and medieval scholarship and the ideas of his contemporaries, for example,
Habermas and **Derrida**. This engagement with the whole gamut of the
history of philosophy is not idle pedantry but part of the general strategy for
approaching questions and problems within **philosophical hermeneutics**.
For Gadamer, although philosophical questions will invariably be particular
and embedded within a specific historical period and problematic, they will,
at the same time, throw light on later – and earlier – formulations of an
issue. Philosophical questions are open to constant re-interpretations. The
ways philosophical questions are formulated in the present are as a result
of the ways problems have been conceptualized in the past. The **effective
history** of a philosophical question means that its current formulation will
be informed by the history of the interpretations and re-evaluations of the
question. Gadamer endorses the Hegelian dictum that philosophy is the
history of philosophy and the history of philosophy is philosophy. The history
of philosophy is not a lifeless catalogue or chronology of dead thinkers; it
is a body of ideas that constitutes a conversational partner in a constantly
active and changing narrative.

Horizon   (See **'fusion of horizons'**.)

Huizinga, Johan (1872–1945)   Johan Huizinga was a Dutch historian,
known for his pioneering work in the development of what is now termed
cultural history. His celebrated work *Homo Ludens* ('Playful Man') was first
published in English in 1949. It is best understood through its subtitle, 'A
study of the play element in culture'. This work brings out the dimension
of **play** at the heart of human civilizations and treats it as a cultural, as
opposed to a biological or psychological, phenomenon.

Huizinga is of significance for the notion of **play**, and his treatment of it in relation to **language** and art is the inspiration for Gadamer's increasing use of the term, firstly in relation to art in Part One of *Truth and Method*, and also much of the later work where play is taken to be an essential part of language and hermeneutical **understanding**. Gadamer acknowledges his debt to Huizinga as one of the sources for his development of the notion of **play**. (See **play**.)

Husserl, Edmund (1859–1938) The founder of the philosophical movement known as **Phenomenology**. Gadamer's relationship to Husserl is a difficult thing to assess. While he regularly refers to Husserl, there are only a handful of texts which are explicitly dedicated to the founder of phenomenology or to the phenomenological movement as such. That said, Gadamer's use of 'horizon', 'fusion', 'part and whole', 'pre-theoretical lived experience', and his reference to the 'life-world' as the fundamental (and forgotten) presupposition underlying all scientific knowledge, owe much to Husserlian phenomenology. However, it should be noted that while Gadamer did read Husserl, he was more influenced by Plato, Aristotle, Hegel and Heidegger, to mention but four key figures. One of the points of contention that Gadamer had with Husserl (and this shows his lasting fidelity to **Hegel** and **Heidegger**) revolves around the question of the historical subject and historical intersubjectivity, over against Husserl's brand of pure (not-mundane) transcendental subjectivity and intersubjectivity. Moreover, Gadamer held that Husserl's account of self-givenness and subjectivity had forgotten the importance of the historical situatedness of interpretation, and that perceptual experience is already run through with a practical-linguistic, i.e. interpretative, interest. One of Gadamer's main criticisms stems from the fact that Husserl held fast to an overtly radicalized Cartesian account of the subject, an in principle self-transparent subject, albeit of the non-empirical kind, in which the very concept of life becomes alienated from itself and falls away from itself. It is precisely in Hegel's historical-dialectical method and Heidegger's hermeneutics of facticity that Gadamer finds a response to Husserl on the intimately dialogical connection between the transcendent reality of the world and our lived, conversational reflection upon this reality. In fact, and perhaps against the very nature of **phenomenology** traditionally conceived, Gadamer's later writing claims that when one reflects on the true nature of linguistic experience, one already moves beyond **subjectivity** and **intersubjectivity**.

— I —

Idealism   Idealism, broadly construed, is the school of thought that does not accept the existence of things outside the mind. It argues that everything comes to be by means of the constitutive subject, i.e. reality is mental or spiritual. Idealism can be either objective if the idea of reality is pure and transcendent, and therefore the guarantor of the world we experience (Plato), and subjective (modern) if the idea is productively posited by the mind and therefore coextensive with the world.

The first complete form of idealism is Platonic idealism, where the idea of reality as immaterial substance over against which the sensible world is only a lack or limitation. Neo-Platonism also presents an idealistic vision of the world in which the enactment of being stems from a pure ontological negativity, i.e. the productive, immaterial no-thing of reality.

In the modern era, Descartes, Kant and finally Fichte established the thinking subject as the absolute centre of all meaning and truth, not only metaphysical, but also ethical and aesthetic. Subsequently, with Schelling's and Hegel's idealism, the coincidence of subject and object, of thought and being, of rational and real, emerges, and finally, the Hegelian synthesis can be considered the most complete form of idealism, with the total resolution of conceptuality and reality through the development of historical Spirit.

Through his readings of Plato, Aristotle and Hegel, Gadamer proposes the integration of natural science and philosophical speculation, arguing that a hermeneutics of the science of Spirit leads us to the problematic dimension of classical metaphysics. And here hermeneutics (and its method of interpretation) becomes both practical philosophy and metaphysics, thanks to the study of the science of Spirit exhibited through the work of art or the ancient texts from which it is possible to draw out philosophical truth. Yet from the standpoint of hermeneutics, dialogue with a work of art acquires new life. As such, dialogue becomes an event that takes place between historically situated partners who know no certainty as to the outcome of their situated interpretation and dialogue.

Inspired by both Plato and Hegel, Gadamer stresses the positive role of the heritage of German idealism and especially the Hegelian brand. His own ties with the issue of Hegelianism explain why the goal of Gadamer's **philosophical hermeneutics** is nonetheless oriented towards a universal method that could embrace every field. Yet nobody understood better than Gadamer that consciousness and its object are not two separate realms, but rather inseparably belong together as parts of a whole. Gadamer rejects both a pure, positing subjectivity or a pure objectivity as a dogmatism of thought. While Hegel's critical faith in reason remains a constant for Gadamer, he argues that the ambitious culmination of idealism led to the covering over of the event of truth and to the emphasis being placed on the cognitive and willing subject.

Ultimately one could say that Gadamer's **philosophical hermeneutics** is trying to subvert the simple binary distinction between idealism and realism, and that Gadamer is attempting to inhabit that space between phenomenology and dialectic; that space between pure language and pure insight, between dialectic and intuition, between word and concept.

Ideology critique   (See **Habermas**.)

The 'Inner word'   (See **Augustine**.)

Interpretation   (See **Understanding**.)

Intersubjectivity   (See **Subjectivity**.)

—K—

Kant, Immanuel, (1724–1804)   Kant is the most important German philosopher of the modern period. He was born in Könisgsberg, then East Prussia now the Russian controlled Kaliningrad. He spent most of his life in this provincial city where he was educated, became a private tutor, and eventually was made professor of philosophy. Kant's work is divided into two distinct phases the first of which is known as the 'Pre-Critical period', which preceded the more influential Critical period. The Pre-Critical period was typical of much of the work of the mid eighteenth century engaging with contemporary philosophers in Germany, France, and Britain. The work of the Critical period was a radical departure and was expounded in Kant's three celebrated 'critiques'; *The Critique of Pure Reason* (1781), *The Critique of Practical Reason* (1788), and the *Critique of Judgement* (1790). Together these works on knowledge, morality, and art, respectively, constitute an elaborate and complex investigation into their foundations and limits. These works are critical in the sense that they define the boundaries of legitimate thought although the term Critical philosophy became simple shorthand for Kantianism, the philosophy of Kant.

The Critique of Judgement brings together the other two critical works. It is divided into two sections, the first part is on aesthetic theory and the second on the role of teleology in nature: the connection between the two parts is not immediately evident. Of aesthetic theory Kant covers such topics as the nature of the sublime, beauty in nature and art and the *sensus communis* (common sense).

Gadamer makes substantial use of Kant's philosophy, especially the *Critique of Judgement*. In the modern period, the status of art as a form of truth is under attack from a new direction. Paradoxically, with the development of the newly created discipline called aesthetics in the eighteenth century, Gadamer sees an implicit attack upon the idea of art as truth once again. Kant's Third Critique (*The Critique of Judgement*), an extremely influential contribution to debates about the nature of art, works on the assumption that art is fundamentally concerned with feeling. For Gadamer, this constitutes an essential 'subjectivisation' of art, for art is reduced to some variety of personal experience and thus fails to rise above the level of feeling. In order to associate art with the more ennobled truth, Gadamer needs to be able to show that art is capable of something of greater significance than the power to engender delight or terror. Ultimately, in claiming truth for art, Gadamer aims to change the emphasis away from the aesthetic consumer to the nature of the artistic product itself, and what that artefact is able to disclose or open up.

Koselleck, Reinhart (1923–)   Reinhart Koselleck is Professor of the Theory of History at the University of Bielefeld and author of *Futures Past: On the Semantics of Historical Time* and *The Practice of Concept History*. He was a student of Gadamer's, and together in the 1950s they edited a journal of concept history (entitled the *Archiv für Begriffsgeschichte*).

Kratz, Frida (1898–1979)   Frida Kratz was Gadamer's first wife. They married in 1923 and Frida gave birth to their daughter, Jutta, in 1926.

Language (See **linguisticality**.)

Language and thought The nature of the relationship between language and thought is a problematic one. A longstanding belief in philosophy takes language to be no more than the vehicle through which thoughts are transmitted; this view is as old as the ancient Greeks. On this view, thought precedes language, and the ability to operate linguistic symbols, to write, to engage in conversation, is secondary to the ability to think. It is the power of thought that gives rise to the ability to communicate in language. But if this sketch of the connection between thinking and language is accurate, it gives rise to the notion of pure thought, a wordless thought that lacks any identifiable linguistic form. Gadamer's conception of language, similar to that of the Austrian philosopher of language, **Ludwig Wittgenstein**, rejects such a formulation. In the celebrated phrase 'being that can be understood is language', Gadamer prioritizes language over thought rather than thought over language. The possibility of any comprehension of being is invariably linguistic in form; this is Gadamer's position and it is at the heart of his herme-neutical account of language. (See also **Wittgenstein**, and **language**.)

Lekebusch, Käte (1921–) Käte Lekebusch was born in Wuppertal, Germany, the daughter of a textile mill owner. She studied philosophy in Leipzig and became Gadamer's research assistant. She was briefly imprisoned in 1944 for denouncing Hitler; the charge was dropped because of insufficient evidence. She became Gadamer's second wife in Frankfurt in 1950 and gave birth to their daughter, Andrea, in 1965.

Linguisticality (and Language) For Gadamer, *logos* is the medium through which human beings and the world meet, or rather the manner in which they appear in their original co-belonging. Moreover, it is in our linguisticality (*Sprachlichkeit*), a concept which Gadamer later concretized, that Gadamer sees the form of experience which is faithful to our finitude, insofar as it articulates the silent and inner potential of language (the capacity to make signs and symbols) and thus puts the historical finite human being in communion with itself, with others and with the world.

With this notion, Gadamer attempted to shed light on the commonality of all modes of understanding. On the one hand, he tried to clarify the ways in which the human being understands himself and his world through language, and on the other, he attempted to unravel the problem and potential of the *logos* (with all the conceptual sedimentation contained within this classical Greek term) as belonging to the question of being and truth. Indeed, the starting point of Gadamer's **philosophical hermeneutics** is the human experience of the linguisticality of the *logos* and not simply man as the experiencing agent. As such, the pages of **Truth and Method** contain a profound ontological reflection on language as the ultimate foundation for an understanding of being. More precisely, it is only by means of language that Being can be understood.

For Gadamer, then, man's experience of the world is always linguistic, yet language is not just a faculty that men possess, but rather, it is because of language that everyone has a world in the first place. Language, however, is not intended as a means of communication, but instead as communication itself in its lived unfolding. Hence language is something absolute and is identified with the horizon of world, insofar as the world is given only in and as language. Language is thus not identified with either the subject or the object, but with the co-belonging of I and world. Following Heidegger, man is thrown into language and, more than merely having it or possessing it, is in reality possessed by it. Gadamer's understanding of language does not reduce language to a set of signs or symbols because our experience of the world is synonymous with our experience of language, insofar as we see and read the world by means of the word. Furthermore, language is not an instrument because it is not ours to use freely to assign meaning, but an ontological structure that lies before us and is thrown beneath us. Gadamer sums up his work and his 'philosophy of language', by saying that we have world and self-understanding only thanks to language and that 'being that can be understood' is language. This enigmatic phrase means that intelligible experience is possible due to the ontological structures of language, which ensure that this experience comes to understanding, is enacted and is given voice therein. Our relationship with the world is given in terms of understanding and interpretation, and these two interwoven strands are always mediated by language. In a word, language underwrites man's understandingly interpretative relationship with the world.

Language, or more concretely the linguisticality of the human being, is what distinguishes the human from the animal, insofar as it enables one to share with others one's inner self and to participate in the inner life of others. However, the Greek concept of *logos* not only refers to the living word as an expression of the human being's linguistic capacity – which is often translated with the Latin word *verbum* – but also the unfolding of rationality and thought through language. It is this meaning which has prevailed in the Latin translation of Aristotle's definition of man as a rational animal, obscuring, according to Gadamer, the linguisticality of human experience, which is intimately tied to rationality, yet not simply reducible to it. Hence, Gadamer stresses the centrality of linguisticality in the process of human development and experience as a whole.

With the capacity to talk about what has yet to be, the human being not only differentiates himself from the animals but also frees himself from his immediate surroundings and frees himself for nature. Thus, for Gadamer, human freedom is intrinsically tied to linguisticality, insofar as the power of language allows humans to transcend their common concerns and to plan their actions for the future, i.e. to reach out towards the most diverse purposes and goals. Consequently the philosophical questions that come to mind – the relationship between being, beings and world – are opened up by language and grounded in our everyday understanding of language. Thus understanding, language, being and world are deeply intertwined and it is the linguisiticality of our experience of the world that testifies to this. Underlying this notion of linguisticality – linguisticality as the power of the inner and as yet unspoken word – is the infinite task of finding one's way in and by means of language, of attempting to bring the unsaid to articulation, to risk misunderstanding in the face of the other, and to let the matter speak its truth. As Gadamer puts it:

> 'Genuinely speaking one's mind has little to do with a mere explication and assertion of our prejudices; rather, it risks our prejudices – it exposes oneself to one's own doubt as well as to the rejoinder of the other. Who has not had the experience – especially before the other whom we want to persuade – of how the reasons that one had for one's view, and even the reasons that speak against one's view, rush into words? The mere presence of the other before whom we stand helps us to break up our own bias and narrowness, even before he opens his mouth to make a reply' ('Text and Interpretation' p. 26).

Linguistic idealism   **Habermas** and other critics make the accusation that Gadamer embraces a position known as linguistic idealism. Because of a failure to recognize the materiality of language and its intimate involvement with practical activities from which it ultimately springs, (a view of language familiar within the Marxist tradition), Gadamer, it is claimed, gives to language a mysterious, even mystical, self-transformative power and hence is guilty of a form of idealism about language.

***Literature and Philosophy in Dialogue* (1994, English only edition)**   Subtitled 'Essays in German Literary Theory' this work is a collection of essays by Gadamer on some of the principal figures in modern German letters. The main essays are philosophical readings of the works of Hölderlin, Goethe and Rainer Maria Rilke.

'Logic of question and answer' (versus formal logic)   **R. G. Collingwood** devised the '**logic of question and answer**' and this was taken over by Gadamer. It is a procedure for working within the human sciences, specifically the practice of understanding historical texts. It works on the general idea that to understand what anyone says always requires going beyond mere utterances to grasp what inspired them (and this is unstated). It rejects the ordinary formal logic, the logic of statements, in favour of a logic of questions. For Collingwood and Gadamer, every text is an answer to a question. To understand a text properly is to uncover the question or questions that motivated it. This is not a question of a psychological investigation into the mind of the author but a matter of serious historical investigation to contextualize the circumstances of a works production. Gadamer claims that Collingwood's version of **the logic of question and answer** was inadequate because it failed to account for the historicity of the interpreter. Collingwood acted on the assumption that the meaning of an event or a text was fixed, and once the fundamental question or questions motivating the text were disclosed, the full meaning of the text became apparent. For Gadamer, the meaning of the text or event is not fixed and he rejects the idea that historical reclamation will disclose true meaning. Such a position neglects the fact that the interpreter of an event or text brings to bear his or her own historical **prejudices**; this Collingwood fails to appreciate.

—M—

McDowell, John (1942–)   South African philosopher with extensive influence within the philosophy of mind and language. Under the influence of **Richard Rorty**, McDowell in '*Mind and World*' (1994) refutes what he perceives as a naturalist reduction prevalent within contemporary philosophy. McDowell instead applies Gadamer's distinction between environment and world, and the concept of 'second nature' to argue for a conceptuality irreducible to biological mechanisms that is present in all our interactions with the world. His key works are: *Mind and World* (1994); *Meaning, Knowledge, and Reality* (1998); and *Mind, Value, and Reality* (1998).

'Masters of suspicion'   (See **hermeneutics of suspicion**.)

Matter at issue *(die Sache)*   The nature of Gadamer's repeated analysis of the matter at issue or the motivating concerns of **philosophical herme-neutics** is fiendishly difficult to put one's finger on. However, it is perhaps important to point out that Gadamer repeatedly stresses that the wonder of all wonders is that understanding emerges against the horizon of communal meaning and participation in that meaning, and at the end of all this meaning and participation one does not simply find a general consensus, but rather a coming to agreement with regard to the 'matter at issue' via the unfolding or working out of multiple, self-critical interpretations. It is this communal dedication to the 'matter at issue' that Gadamer sees as being demonstrated in the play of question and answer, and it is the activity of the conversation partners which is at the service of giving voice to the fundamental ontological structure of the matter which motivates questioning in the first place.

While Gadamer has fought long and hard to defend himself against the charge of a certain pan-linguisticism, one could be forgiven for thinking that language seems to become 'the matter' of thinking itself. The fact is that, for Gadamer, Being, understanding and language are so completely interwoven that it is hard to examine the 'matter at issue' without immediately and neces-sarily connecting it to language. However, it is probably wise to remember that Gadamer connects the 'matter at issue' to what is as yet unsaid, and as such it is a task of getting back behind what is said. Thus speaking necessarily carries with it the unsaid of linguisticality, which points to what Gadamer indicates as 'the living virtuality of speech that brings a totality of meaning into play, without being able to express it totally' (*TM*, p. 458). All in all, while the 'matter at issue' is not directly related to the spoken word, it is inconceivable that Gadamer would not have indexed it to linguisticality or to the virtuality of a speaking which is contained in the promise of a word yet to come.

Meaning versus significance   (See **Hirsch**.)

Medical science   (See **Enigma of Health**.)

Method   For the modern age, the search for a method is part of the quest for truth. The assumption that an appropriate method gives access to certainty and truth is the legacy of **Descartes**. One of the principal aims of Gadamer's *Truth and Method* is to combat this orthodoxy; far from disclosing truth, he argues, method does in fact obscure and distort it. Part of the illusion of method is its alleged universal applicability. The role of the observer, and the particularity and specificity of the situation are necessary component parts in the procedure of understanding and they militate against the mechanical application of a method. The purpose of *Truth and Method* is to demonstrate that there is, within the philosophical tradition, a richer account of truth than that which is disclosed by the application of a strict method. The principal themes of art, history and language in *Truth and Method* are actually aspects of truth that cannot be disclosed in a methodologically conducted way. Part of Gadamer's argument in *Truth and Method* is that the procedures of natural science (*Naturwissenschaft*) are inappropriate to the subject matter of the human sciences (*Geisteswissenschaft*). This was a central insight of **Wilhelm Dilthey**, one of the key figures in nineteenth century **hermeneutics**, for whom understanding was the objective of the human sciences whereas explanation was the objective of the natural sciences.

Mill, John Stuart (1806–1873)   English philosopher and politician noted for his work in many areas of philosophy, including philosophy of science, logic, ethics and political philosophy. His publications include: *A System of Logic* (1843), *On Liberty* (1859) and *Utilitarianism* (1863). He was an early champion of feminism and his *Subjection of Women* (1869), co-written with his partner Harriet Taylor Mill, is an established classic in the genre of feminist literature. Mill's *On Liberty* is one of the most important political tracts of the nineteenth century and is seen by many as the most important theoretical justification of liberalism. Mill's liberalism is fabricated upon the basic premise that all assertions are fallible. Within political life this amounts to an obligation to accept all possible views and shades of opinion as valid. Put another way, no opinion or point of view is automatically discounted as unacceptable. On the other hand, all views are to be open to public scrutiny and debate and need to be vigorously challenged and held to account. On this view there is no absolute truth, for history shows how accepted views are, over time, rejected and superseded.

Gadamer clearly knew the work of Mill, as the opening chapter of **Truth and Method** demonstrates. What is most striking is the fact that Gadamer's work shares many of the qualities of Mill's liberalism. Mill denies the possibility of absolute truth because assertions and opinions can – and always will be – open to question: to assume a position to be so self-evidently true as to be unchallengeable is to lapse into dogmatism. Mill derives from this a politics of pluralism and toleration; no views are to be automatically outlawed and a general tolerance of the views of others is a prerequisite of a liberal polity. Tolerance is not mere passive acceptance of views one finds antithetical or repugnant; the price one pays for the holding of views, especially unpopular ones, is that one is obliged to defend such views by way of **dialogue** and debate. This position is remarkably similar to the account of truth operating within **philosophical hermeneutics**.

—N—

National Socialism   Unlike his teacher and mentor, **Martin Heidegger**, Gadamer did not join the National Socialist (Nazi) party despite staying in Germany throughout the time of Hitler's Third Reich. After the Second World War Gadamer did not undergo the process of denazification; in fact he was promoted to Rector of his university in Leipzig, in communist East Germany. In recent years Gadamer's relationship to the Nazis has been re-examined in the light of the work of various modern critics who have sought to suggest that Gadamer was closer to National Socialism than he was prepared to admit. A black mark against him, according to his critics, is the fact that he did not show his abhorrence for the Hitler regime by emigrating; he stayed in Germany throughout the war period. He engaged in 'inner emigration', that is, he silently kept his head down and kept quiet while intellectually refusing to give the regime credence or respectability. In interviews Gadamer claimed that he was able to continue as an academic because the Nazis did not see philosophers as a threat to the regime.

Against this generally accepted picture of Gadamer's non-involvement with the Nazis during the war years, recent controversial studies – of questionable academic worth it has to be said – suggest a murkier past. Certain critics claim that his activities during the Third Reich indicate a closer relationship to Nazism than he ever admitted publicly. The case against him depends upon the following claims made about his activities during the Nazi period. He gained professorial positions, it is claimed, by unscrupulously taking over posts of 'furloughed', i.e. sacked, academics of Jewish descent. For example, he accepted the professorship to replace Richard Kroner, the Jewish professor at Kiel. It is asserted that he attended a Nazi summer school for university teachers. He is accused of giving a lecture on Herder (the 'father of German nationalism') in Paris during the occupation. Finally, his 1934 essay 'Plato and the poets' succoured fascist notions of the state, and in some way contributed to ideological support for the Nazi regime.

Richard Palmer, a former student of Gadamer's and a leading exponent of **philosophical hermeneutics** in North America, has challenged the claims about his teacher's dubious record during the Nazi period and his intellectual and practical closeness to Nazism. Palmer's view is that the attacks upon Gadamer are largely spurious because there is no evidence to support them. In later life Gadamer spoke very little about the Nazi years so to some extent the jury is still out as those attacking Gadamer rely on conjecture. One suspects it will involve a good deal of further historical work to get a more accurate picture.

Natorp, Paul (1854–1924) Paul Natorp's influence on Gadamer, specifically in his reading of Plato, was significant, and Gadamer wrote his doctoral dissertation, entitled *The Nature of Pleasure in Plato's Dialogues*, under the supervision of the Marburg neo-Kantian in 1922. Natorp influenced Gadamer's interpretation of Plato's *Philebus* on the relationship between reason and pleasure and Natorp proposed a Kantianized interpretation of Plato's theory of ideas, and, in general, both men had strong ontological and epistemological interpretations of Plato. Gadamer's view was ontological, while Natorp's was more epistemological. Gadamer's interpretation of Plato's philosophy, even in its early stages, was far removed from Natorp's epistemologically driven method. Plato's so-called 'theory of Ideas', for example, is considered by Natorp to be the heart of Platonism, albeit not as transcendent forms, while according to Gadamer, a 'theory of ideas' did not strictly even exist: it had been attributed to Plato by Aristotle and, after him, by a long philosophical tradition which had subsequently extracted a reductively unilateral two-world theory or doctrine from the various dialogues. According to Gadamer, and perhaps under the influence of the Tübingen School's interest in Plato's 'Unwritten Doctrines', the truth of the Ideas, and our recollective participation in them, is to be found in the reality of lived conversation and in the playful and dramatic nature of the dialogues.

However, it should be noted that Gadamer came to admire, albeit late in his own career, the speculative nature of Natorp's own late philosophy of language and the latter's own attempt to articulate the relationship between the mystery of language and the happening of meaning through understanding. It is precisely with this insight that philosophical hermeneutics (and perhaps with it the late Natorp) becomes genuinely ontological. As such, both Gadamer and the late Natorp argue that the meaning of being always shines through or comes to articulation in and through language.

Nietzsche, Friedrich, (1844–1900)   German philosopher born near Leipzig, the son of a Lutheran minister. Precociously talented, he studied at the universities of Bonn and Leipzig and became a Professor of Philology in Basel, Switzerland, at the age of twenty-four. Ill health forced him to resign his position in 1879 and he spent the next ten years in a nomadic existence, moving between France, Germany and Italy. He suffered a final mental breakdown in 1889 and spent the next eleven years of his life as an invalid, never fully regaining his health and sanity. Of his works, including essays and aphorism, the most notable are *Beyond Good and Evil* (1886), *The Genealogy of Morals* (1887) and the posthumously published *The Will to Power*. Nietzsche is proclaimed by many as one of the principal precursors of postmodernism. His work represents a powerful critique of the established accounts of knowledge and truth and his work challenges the foundations of traditional religious and ethical thought in the western tradition. Nietzsche had a profound influence upon Gadamer's teacher, **Martin Heidegger**.

—**O**—

Objectivity   (See **Subjectivity**.)

Ontology   For Gadamer, language plays an indispensable role in the process of ontological disclosure and it does so by essentially opening up the question of being. Being comes to expression in language and is comprehensible only by means of language. That ontology is necessarily hermeneutic means that philosophy rejects the possibility of any immediate intuition or apprehension of being as identical in its self-presentation, and accepts the need to understand what manifests itself by means of language. Hence language is a mark of finitude insofar as it opens up the process of human understanding and allows us to makes sense of what presents itself. **Philosophical hermeneutics** is a philosophy that acknowledges its finitude and admits to being destined to an understanding of being which must always offer a new account of itself which challenges our non-understanding. This is why the ontological turn in Gadamer's hermeneutics never sees itself as the final word or the definitive answer, but rather opens itself up to the next question.

   The ontology of language that Gadamer develops is in part motivated by Heidegger's destruction or dismantling of the history of ontology and, as such, Gadamer's critique of the modern subject and the limits and excesses of modernity are central to his linguistic-ontological turn. The solution he proposes to find a real way out of the impasse that has led to post-Cartesian philosophy starts from the overlooked experience of language as already overcoming the forced dichotomy between subject and object. From the beginning, the space in which Gadamer's ontology moves is very limited: the epistemological horizon of the problem of modernity, which examines the multiplicity of being, reducing them to being as true or false, as simply present or absent. In a word, Gadamer argues that one cannot even conceive of an experience of truth that transcends the limits of linguistic mediation. If there is no human experience that escapes the linguistic nexus, then one cannot 'speak' of the extra-linguistic experience. In short, this is the basis of Gadamer's famously enigmatic phrase 'being that can be understood is language' (*Sein, das verstehen werden kann, ist Sprache*, **TM**, p. 141). One could argue that this absolutization of the *logos* ends in a paradoxical way by replacing Hegel's absolute Spirit – self-consciousness and absolute-reflection – but with opposite characteristics: a non-subjective reflection which is always mediated by language. As such, being is precisely what emerges in linguistic comprehension because being presents itself to understanding and the being of understanding comes to word. Language, or better linguisticality, is the process of being coming into language.

Ultimately, Gadamer denies man's ability to transcend the finitude of his experience of being, and this has implications for his understanding of the human being: the human being and his/her life-world are dissolved in the story of the ongoing creative process of logos. There is no being proper to man for man is only the site of the manifestation of the *logos*. Using Gadamer's own metaphor, language plays with us and plays through us. The freedom that Gadamer recognizes in man, a freedom which is grounded in the **linguisticality** of his being, is potentially complicated by the persistent feeling that man's freedom is always conditioned by how he responds to the **play** of language or the mediated meaning of being through language.

The Origin of the Work of Art   First published in Germany in 1950, *The Origin of the Work of Art* is the title of a series of lectures **Martin Heidegger** gave in the 1930s in Zurich and Frankfurt. Heidegger is sharply critical of the subjectivization and aestheticization of art. He advances the radical view that art is fundamental to our being for it grounds and discloses a culture's self-conception, its truth. To illustrate his point Heidegger uses, among others, the examples of a painting of a pair of shoes by Vincent van Gogh and a Greek temple. Gadamer was present at these lectures and they were profoundly influential in the formation of his own account of art as truth. Gadamer also wrote the Introductory essay to the German edition of this work. (See **aesthetics**.)

— P —

Parmenides (515–450 BCE)   A **Pre-Socratic philosopher** and founder
of the Eleatic school of Greek philosophy (relating to the ancient Greek city
of Elea in south west Italy). Parmenides denied the possibility of change in
the world, arguing that movement presupposed an impossible shift from
being to non-being.

Phenomenology   Gadamer's relationship to phenomenology, Gadamer's
phenomenological credentials if you will, are fundamental to any understanding of Gadamer's philosophical hermeneutics, and his work 'The
Phenomenological Movement' (contained in Philosophical Hermeneutics)
displays both a fidelity to and distance from Husserlian and Heideggerian
forms of phenomenological thinking. The Phenomenological Movement first
appeared in 1963 in the journal Philosophische Rundschau and it undoubtedly
represents his most relevant points of engagement with Husserlian phenomenology and its determining influence on his hermeneutical project. In a
later telling remark he writes: 'What one now calls hermeneutical philosophy
is based to a large extent on phenomenology' (Heidegger's Ways, p. 51).
With Heidegger's immanent critique of Husserlian phenomenology, hermeneutics assumed genuine philosophical significance, shifting from the simple
confines of an epistemological and methodological orientation still present
in **Dilthey**'s work. In Being and Time the real question was no longer
conceived as the way in which being is grasped, but rather the way in which
linguistic understanding and being belong together. As Gadamer has it, this
motivated Heidegger to argue that understanding is not simply a subjective
attitude or faculty, but a fundamental mode of existence that 'denotes the
basic being-in-motion of Dasein that constitutes its finitude and historicity,
and hence embraces the whole of its experience of the world' (**TM**, XXVII).

Prior to the publication of **Truth and Method**, Gadamer gave a series of
lectures in 1957–58 at the Catholic University of Leuven in which he sees
in Husserlian phenomenology, specifically Husserl's later analysis of the life-
world, the virtue of having twisted free from the strictures of neo-Kantian
methodology and of having opened up the entirety of our experience of the
world, which is not reducible to the causal nexus of the natural objective
sciences. Also Husserl's attempt to reclaim and thematize the pre-categorial

and pre-predicative, i.e. evidential, experience of the life-world was also seen by Gadamer as a radical attempt to win back a much overlooked field of historical experience that had been buried by the ideal and universalistic pretensions of the sciences of consciousness. Here Gadamer points to the proximity between **Husserl**'s analysis of the historical life-world and **Dilthey**'s 'critique of historical reason', insofar as the latter, according to Gadamer, responded to **Kant**'s *Critique of Pure Reason* by stating that just like the objective sciences, consciousness itself is historically determined and its historically sedimented motivations need to be uncovered.

However, beyond the radical critique of scientism and objectivism found in previous philosophy, it is difficult to bring together Husserl's account of the life-world with **Heidegger**'s hermeneutically inspired phenomenology, insofar as Husserl's *Crisis of the European Sciences*, potentially inspired by Heidegger's criticisms, was unable – or better, unwilling – to abandon the transcendental-egological dimension and his dream of philosophy as a rigorous science. Gadamer did not reject out of hand the historical nature of Husserl's account of the life-world but he does seems to have had a preference for Heidegger's analysis of *Dasein*'s thrownness into a historical world or his 'hermeneneutics of facticity'. The motivation behind Gadamer's Heideggerian preference stems from the Cartesian detachment or the non-participating subject put forward by Husserl in the guise of the phenomenological-transcendental reduction, and it is precisely the apodictic evidence of a constituting consciousness, intended as a foundational principle and a universal and concrete field of transcendental experience, which Gadamer finds problematic when it comes to mapping the terrain of a genuine philosophical analysis of lived experience as it plays itself out through a historical process. It is Heidegger's 'hermeneutics of facticity' that promises to address this concern. As such, Husserl's *Crisis* represents not a movement towards Heidegger's way of thinking but rather a defensive movement which offers a response to some of Heidegger's criticisms.

However, Gadamer was deeply convinced that Heidegger's work does not amount to a destruction of Husserlian phenomenology, but instead its broadening, writing:

> '... what constituted the significance of Heidegger's funda-
> mental ontology was not that is was the solution to the prob-
> lem of historicism, and certainly not a more original grounding

of science, nor even, as with Husserl, philosophy's ultimate radical grounding of itself; rather, the whole idea of grounding itself underwent a total reversal. It was no longer with the same intention as Husserl that Heidegger undertook to interpret being, truth and history in terms of absolute temporality. For this temporality was not that of 'consciousness' nor of the transcendental Ur-I. ... Heidegger's thesis was that being itself is time. This burst asunder the whole subjectivism of modern philosophy – and, in fact, as was soon to appear, the whole horizon of questions asked by metaphysics, which tended to define being as what is present' (**TM**, pp. 247–8).

The innovative importance of Heidegger's early project cannot be found in his critique of the insufficiently ontological nature of Husserl's concept of consciousness, the being of intentional consciousness, and the metaphysical suppositions still operative therein. With the term *Dasein* Heidegger is attempting to think differently about the way of being of the human being and critically to subvert concepts such as subjectivity, self-consciousness and transcendental egoity. Hence Heidegger's famous statement 'the essence of *Dasein* lies in its existence' (*Being and Time*, p. 67) means that there is a priority and irreducibility to the singularity of existence and so the real task of philosophy is to shed light on the temporality and historicality of the constitutively finite manner of human existence and the ontological significance of the human being's way of understanding itself and the meaning of being.

In *Being and Time*, and in his earlier lectures from 1925, Heidegger began to question the entire Husserlian project and demanded an entirely new and more original understanding of the phenomenological method which would remain mindful of the **historicity** of human experience and its bearing on the question of the meaning of being. As such, Husserl's maxim 'to the things themselves!' took on an entirely different sense for Heidegger as he put in question the very nature of 'the things themselves' and our mode of access to these things which remain, for the most part, hidden from the history of philosophy. It is precisely the question of the meaning of being and later the truth of being that becomes the 'matter' for thinking. However, Gadamer still maintained that Heidegger remained a phenomenologist even after the so-called 'turn' in his thinking, which brought Heidegger further and further away from the transcendental concerns of *Being and Time*, i.e.

the question of the meaning of being, to his later meditation on the role and nature of language and its relation to the truth of being.

It is perhaps in Heidegger's later meditation on language that Gadamer's concern becomes most evident, insofar as our experience of things, our experience of having a world and the nature of language become deeply interwoven phenomena. As Gadamer has it:

> 'Language and thinking about things are so bound together
> that it is an abstraction to conceive of the system of truths as a
> pregiven system of possibilities of being for which the signifying
> subject selects corresponding signs. A word is not a sign that one
> selects, nor is it a sign that one makes or gives to another; it is
> not an existent thing that one picks up and gives an ideality of
> meaning in order to make another being visible through it. This is
> mistaken on both counts. Rather, the ideality of the meaning lies
> in the word itself. … Experience is not wordless to begin with,
> subsequently becoming an object of reflection by being named,
> by being subsumed under the universality of the word. Rather,
> experience of itself seeks and finds words that express it. We seek
> the right word – i.e., the word that really belongs to the thing –
> so that in it the thing comes into language' (**TM**, pp. 416-7).

What Gadamer means here is that word and thing belong together, and by dint of this Gadamer is forced to reject the Husserlian conception of language as a mere expression, the exteriorization of a signification. In reality, it is language and not transcendental consciousness that is the ground of every possible phenomenological designation. For Gadamer, the letting something be seen in its mode of self-givenness, which is the genuine vocation of phenomenology, no longer means the same as it did for Husserl. The thing itself is not a self-given object 'in the flesh', i.e. in the fullness of its intuitive evidence, instead the matter (*Sache*) of philosophy is that about which we try to speak, that which addresses us as a co-respondent, that which is given in and through the event of language as withdrawn and in need of a voice.

Philosophical Apprenticeships   Gadamer did not publish a definitive autobiography, but in 1977 he produced *Philosophical Apprenticeships*, a memoir, focusing on the earlier part of his life. In this work Gadamer gives short sketches of those philosophers and intellectuals who influenced his intellectual development. They range from **Paul Natorp, Max Scheler** and **Martin Heidegger**, his teachers, to **Karl Löwith, Karl Jaspers**, his colleagues and, in some cases, friends. Although Gadamer is outlining his philosophical development the work gives very little away about Gadamer, the man. This was clearly intentional in the light of the book's epigraph: 'Of myself I say nothing', (a phrase taken from the English philosopher Francis Bacon and also used by Immanuel Kant in his *Critique of Pure Reason*). Gadamer seeks to present a picture of himself not by way of a personal assessment of his achievements but through a detailed description of the historical and cultural milieu within which his philosophical outlook was shaped. This emphasis upon context rather than an explanation at the level of subjectivity is of a piece with Gadamer's general hermeneutical approach to philosophy. In 1997 Gadamer produced another autobiographical sketch entitled 'Reflections On My Philosophical Journey'. This essay covers some of the same ground as *Philosophical Apprenticeships* but importantly offers retrospective thoughts on *Truth and Method* in the light of the verdicts of his critics and his own reflections on the strengths and shortcomings of his work. The essay, amongst other things an exercise in self-criticism, also points to the development of themes and ideas in Gadamer's work after *Truth and Method*.

Philosophical Hermeneutics (1967)   This is a collection of thirteen short essays, largely taken from the three-volume collection of Gadamer's early short essays (the *Kleine Schriften*). These works are wide ranging and amplify much of the material from *Truth and Method*.

Philosophical hermeneutics   Since Descartes, modern philosophy regarded correct *method* as a route to absolute certainty. Armed with a rational procedure, human thought becomes equal to natural science in replacing the dark forces of tradition with objective truth. The work of **Gadamer** contests this optimistic account of modernity, especially in the major work *Truth and Method* (1960). Gadamer starts by re-evaluating the idea of **tradition** – from which **Enlightenment** thought distanced itself – claiming that '**tradition**' and 'reason' cannot be so easily teased apart. For Gadamer, tradition cannot be an object of 'pure' rational enquiry. The idea that we can step outside our own cultural reference points to embrace timeless truth is a demonstrable fiction of modernist thought.

Gadamer relates his idea of '**tradition**' to a reworked notion of '**prejudice**', which he understands as pre-judice or pre-judgement, in other words as that which makes any kind of discrimination possible. A **prejudice** is not a distorting form of thought that must be shaken off before we see the world aright. For Gadamer prejudices are present in all understanding. Against **Enlightenment** claims that reason, detached from historical and cultural perspective, gives a test for truth, Gadamer claims that we are irredeemably embedded in language and culture, and that the escape to unclouded certainty via rational method is a chimera.

How does Gadamer substantiate the assertion that forms of understanding are always prejudicial and that we cannot make strictly objective claims about the world? Here is where we find his singular contribution to contemporary thought. Understanding is invariably 'hermeneutical', he claims. The term derives from **_hermeneutics_**, 'the branch of knowledge dealing with interpretation' (_Oxford English Dictionary_). Historically, hermeneutics was the art of correctly reading and interpreting ancient texts, notably the Bible. In Gadamer's hands **hermeneutics** becomes a more general procedure for understanding itself, which he terms **philosophical hermeneutics** and characterizes in terms of a **hermeneutical circle**. The idea of the circle refers to the constantly turning movement between one part of a text and its total meaning. In making sense of a fragment of the text one is always simultaneously interpreting the whole. Gadamer justifies extending the role of hermeneutics, making it a necessary characteristic of any attempt to understand the world, by referring back to the history of hermeneutics and early attempts to codify interpretative practice. Hermeneutics is also a submerged strand running through the history of philosophy. Aristotle's account of _phronesis_ or 'practical wisdom' is a case in point. In becoming moral we are habituated into a moral tradition, Aristotle asserts, but the moral agent is always confronted with situations that go beyond the regularities of habit. This oscillation between habit and novelty is similar to the dynamic of the hermeneutical circle.

Gadamer's principal authority for his claims is his teacher **Martin Heidegger**. In _Being and Time_ Heidegger shows how interpretation of the world is impossible without pre-understanding. Against Descartes, he shows that understanding is not worked out in the privacy of consciousness but through our being in the world. But if all understanding is interpretation, it is still guided by what Gadamer calls a fusion of horizons. A text, or any thing or event within the world we interpret, has its own _horizon_ of meaning. Interpretation is situated within the mutual horizon of the interpreter and the thing to be interpreted.

The modernist thought that understanding depends on a detachment from tradition effected by rational method is undermined when viewed from the hermeneutical perspective. For Gadamer, truth is not method but simply what happens in dialogue. Acts of interpretation are dialogical, part of a ceaseless conversation within tradition. The interpreter projects provisional meanings but these are disturbed and redefined when the interpreter's own prejudices are questioned by the horizon of the text or the partner in dialogue. Ultimately, Gadamer claims, meanings can never be complete.

Another consequence of Gadamer's **fusion of horizons** is a redefined relationship to the past. If all understanding is dialogue, it is as much a conversation with the past as with the future. So the past is not 'another country' but a continuous effect in the present, as contemporary language and that of antiquity work together within a common tradition. Here again the idea of methodological detachment is, for Gadamer, a non-starter. We cannot find an Archimedean point outside culture and language in our pursuit of truth, as our prejudices, the conditions of understanding, are part of what we seek to make comprehensible.

Gadamer's questioning of rational method rejects the view that reason stands behind language. Cultural products (including art) and the natural world are not objects for rational investigation but voices within the fabric of an interminable conversation.

Philosophy   Gadamer's calls his work **philosophical hermeneutics**; this invites the question; How is his version of hermeneutics related to the traditional project of philosophy? His **hermeneutics** is not a general theory of interpretation, nor is it a manual for guiding understanding in the human sciences, but because philosophical hermeneutics concerns itself with the general nature of human understanding, it occupies a space once the domain of philosophy: it is for this reason that Gadamerian hermeneutics is unavoidably philosophical. Philosophy has become a narrow specialism of little concern to other areas of intellectual life and philosophical hermeneutics has little in common with the more technical and recondite aspects of contemporary analytic philosophy. The original task of philosophy, as the ancient Greeks conceived it, for example, was to engage in the most general and wide-ranging enquiry. Over time knowledge has been divided into areas of specific concern and hived off from philosophy: psychology, mathematics, in fact all areas of enquiry were originally aspects of the ancient discipline of philosophy. Gadamer's philosophical hermeneutics, with its claims to universality, offers the possibility of a return to a more unitary and all encompassing mode of enquiry. Gadamer himself applied hermeneutical perspectives to, *inter alia*, literary and philosophical texts, medical science and education. In recent years hermeneutical perspectives have made their mark upon linguistics, sociology and social theory, history, theology and jurisprudence.

Phronesis   *Techne* with regard to production and *phronesis* with regard to action are part of Aristotle's taxonomy of practical activities. Techne, although it is a 'state by virtue of which the soul possesses truth' (*Nicomachean Ethics*, 1139b15), is clearly not the state of knowing appropriate for action because the end of *techne* is production, unlike other states of knowing where the object is an activity. Technical knowledge presupposes the application of rules and techniques with the object of creating something, a clear conception of which is grasped beforehand. Preceding the act of production the agent possesses both knowledge of what is to be made and a firm grasp of the guiding principles and rules to which the object will conform. Success in production is determined by conformity of the procedures to the object.

Concerning moral action there are no hard and fast principles to be drawn upon, nor is there an object to which knowledge should be directed. The good person knows s/he has to act or refrain from acting in a certain way but never reflects in advance upon the appropriate response. Technical knowledge is always for the sake of something else: not so with action. The quality possessed by the good person is *phronesis*, a 'reasoned state or capacity' (Aristotle), or an intuition about the appropriate action to perform (in the light of more general knowledge about the constituents of a good life). The knowledge required for action is intrinsically related to the self-conceptions of the agent and cannot be codified or formulated in terms of principles, nor can it be reduced to a reliable method and be taught. The good person is one disposed to act out of habituation.

Becoming good is a relatively unreflective matter. Habits of character are picked up by following the example of those already in possession of virtue. We are drawn into the moral tradition of desirable actions, generous acts, truthful acts and so forth, but the accumulated habits will not offer guidance as to whether in this particular situation one must choose X or Y. Each situation is utterly unique: its strangeness exposes the inadequacy of general rules. Rules by their very nature can never be programmatically applied to specific cases.

The hermeneutical dimension to phronesis is now explicit in the problem of application. In performing an action I apply my knowledge acquired in the past to the present. *Phronesis* reveals the real structure of understanding; not as a knowing subject grasping an object but as an experience through which the prejudices or habits, passed on in the tradition, encounter the strange and the new. The novelty is not tamed by being classified according to some organizing principle; on the contrary, it is disruptively experienced as it pulls us up short. For example, in deciding what to do, either X or Y, I have no way of knowing whether X or Y are genuinely classifiable as instances of general rules. The habits of everyday morality inform me that I must not lie but is what I am doing *now* lying, or is it something else? And what I am doing *now* is not identical to anything I have ever done before, however similar. This is the sense in which every situation is experienced as both novel and unique. But for all these problems, the person of *phronesis* will know how to proceed since customs and habits by their nature are both flexible and adaptable. On the other hand, explicit rules do not allow for any measure of interpretative negotiation being intrinsically rigid.

Plato (429–347 BCE)   Plato's aporetic dialogues are probably the most significant influence on Gadamer's **philosophical hermeneutics**, and it is in Plato's dialogical '**play**' of question and answer that Gadamer finds his own early inspiration. In fact, Gadamer's *Habilitation* (completed in 1929 under Heidegger's supervision) was dedicated to Plato's *Philebus*, later published under the title of *Plato's Dialectical Ethics* (1931), and his lectures throughout the 1930–40s revolved around ancient Greek philosophy. Gadamer makes it abundantly clear in his *Habilitation* and in his subsequent writings that it is not just Plato's emphasis on the content of the question which inspired him, but rather the ways in which philosophical questions can be formulated and reformulated in the spirit of Plato's philosophy, and that this is also a living issue for contemporary philosophy in terms of hermeneutical conversation. That is to say, the exemplary spirit of goodwill, playful curiosity and risk-taking involved in asking and answering questions is still the yardstick against which Gadamer measures philosophical acumen.

Two of the three major pillars of Platonic philosophy also make up the pillars of philosophical hermeneutics, namely, the Good, the Beautiful and the True, and their bearing on the life of *praxis* is a constant theme in Gadamer's thought. Breaking with the early Heidegger's predilection for Aristotle over Plato, Gadamer sought to return to Plato's dialogues in order to delineate a reading of Plato which would not fall under the Heideggerian category of 'metaphysical thinking' or understand Plato as the original site of the 'forgetting of Being'. Rather than reading Plato as the inauguration of metaphysical thinking, Gadamer chooses to understand the motivating drive of Plato's dialogues as that of awakening our thought to a truth that is already nascent in us as linguistic, conversational beings. Importantly, however, Gadamer refuses to read Plato against Aristotle or Aristotle against Plato, instead referring to the effective unity of thinking or 'unitary effect' (*Wirkungseinheit*) which binds their *logos*-thinking together (*The Idea of the Good*, p. 1). This way Gadamer remains mindful of the co-belonging of Platonic-Aristotelian philosophy and, in doing so, he puts some light between Heidegger's reading of the ancients and his own more historically discerning one.

Another way of understanding the importance of Gadamer's relationship to Plato is to examine his debate with the so-called Tübingen School of Plato interpretation. The Tübingen School, starting with Hans Joachim Krämer (1929–) and Konrad Gaiser (1929–1988), considered Schleiermacher's interpretation of Plato problematic, especially because **Schleiermacher** did not take into account Plato's statements in the *Phaedrus* regarding the primacy of the spoken word over the written, and the various indications that Plato himself left behind in his writings, specifically in the *Seventh Letter*, about the importance of oral teaching that was not made explicit in the dialogues. The statement from the *Seventh Letter*, from which the various proponents of the Tübingen School take their start, is the following: 'Every serious man in dealing with really serious subjects carefully avoids writing' (344c). **Schleiermacher**, according to the Tübingen School, privileged the direct traditional reception of Plato, neglecting an important element in Platonic hermeneutics, represented by what is called *agrapha dogmata*, the unwritten doctrines or dogmas that can be reconstructed through the indirect tradition. Among other things, according to Krämer and Gaiser, Schleiermacher should have understood that the very dialogue form did not simply mean that Plato favoured a literary device designed to combine poetry and philosophy, but, more importantly, the primacy attributed to the dialogue form was intended to emphasize the unique value of oral teaching, which can never be captured in writing. Schleiermacher, according to Krämer and Gaiser, based his interpretation of Plato on two principles: the first was the Lutheran principle of *sola scriptura*, i.e. the absolutization of the text, which led him to focus on the self-sufficiency or independence of the writings themselves, and the other was Schelling's philosophy of identity, which locates a romanticized Plato who stressed the identity between the finite and the infinite.

Gadamer joined the debate and accepted only part of Krämer's and Gaiser's thesis, putting forward an original position of his own which re-evaluates the Tübingen School's reconstruction of Schleiermacher. Gadamer's interpretation is important because it comes from one of the most important contemporary hermeneutic philosophers engaged in a re-reading of the Greeks, and also one of the main proponents of a hermeneutic philosophy of language. Gadamer recognizes that the general problem with interpreting Plato is based on the opaque dialogical relationship between the work itself and teachings of Plato, which can be grasped only through indirect tradition. Still, according to Gadamer, none of the so-called unwritten doctrines, indirectly handed down by the tradition, is in fact absent from the writings of Plato, nor do they even contradict many of the arguments put forward in his written dialogues. Hence these writings, as Schleiermacher advocated, must remain the principle touchstone for a genuinely hermeneutic reading of Plato. Moreover, the fact that Aristotle, the most important student and critic of Plato, does not speak at length of the existence of the unwritten doctrines, nor of the alleged difference between oral and written teaching, is for Gadamer further evidence of the validity of Schleiermacher's thesis. That said, the Tübingen School took the very notion of *agrapha dogmata* from a comment in Aristotle's *Physics*, which states: 'It is true, indeed, that the account he gives there of the participant is different from what he [Plato] says in his so-called unwritten teaching (*agrapha dogmata*)' (*Physics*, Book IV, 209b 12–14).

For his part, then, Gadamer argues that there is a far deeper reason to justify the priority attributed by Schleiermacher to Plato's written work and this is the indissoluble bond established by Plato between **dialogue** and **dialectic**. Starting from the basic thesis expressed in *Truth and Method*, Gadamer argues that Plato's assent to the truth is embodied in the dialogue form itself, and that the dialogue represents, even in its written form, the most complete expression of Platonic dialectic. Moreover, Gadamer argues, it is Schleiermacher who first realized the importance of the unwritten doctrines in Platonic thought, but believed that these doctrines must be understood hermeneutically and from within their written context, and this involves the reader's ability to participate in the life of the text as a living dialogue. The reader has to make the written dialogue a partner in a living conversation, penetrating deeper into the text and understanding its sedimented layers of meaning. Therefore the position put forward by Gadamer in *Truth and Method*, which focuses on the dialogical and dialectical notion of truth and being, refuses to separate the so-called unwritten doctrines from the written dialogues. As such, Plato not only chose the dialogue form but Plato, the author, chose to re-enact the dialogue form in writing so as to give voice to its dialectical character and to do so continually.

Play   Play is a central notion in Gadamer's philosophy. In *Truth and Method* play is a defining characteristic of art and language. Play, as an essential aspect of art, is of great significance for Gadamer. This idea, although important in the tradition of German aesthetic theory, notably in Schiller and Kant and after, does not for Gadamer come directly from these sources. He looks to the anthropological work of the Dutch cultural historian **Johan Huizinga**. Although Huizinga charts the historical importance of play in all aspects of cultural life, Gadamer transforms play into a central feature of art.

What does he mean by play? As well as obvious instances of play in organized sports, Gadamer has in mind the actual phenomenon of play in its endless variety, including metaphorical senses: 'the play of light, the play of the waves, the play of gears or parts of machinery, the interplay of limbs, the play of forces, the play of gnats, even a play on words' (*TM*, p. 103).

Despite their differences, what these aspects of play all share in common is a 'to-and-fro movement that is not tied to any goal that would bring it to an end' (*TM*, p. 103). Play is an activity that is not random and yet has no obvious goal or teleological endpoint; purposeful and yet without some grand overarching purpose. A to-and-fro movement is evident in all ball games where the ball is constantly in motion, providing the character of the play itself. No one knows how the game will end: it is given to sudden reversals of fortune, to the element of surprise as it shocks and unsettles expectations. Play is not necessarily light-hearted, as it clearly is in the operation of pastimes; in fact play can often start as a simple diversion and suddenly become deadly serious when winning or losing becomes a 'matter of life and death', as we say, albeit metaphorically, but with serious intent. Play is a constant to-and-fro movement and Gadamer focuses on this incessant back and forth motion because it reveals something about the nature of art as being essentially incomplete and incompletable. The meaning of artworks is what is revealed and opened up in the constant oscillation between artwork and interpreter. The meaning of the artwork is never final, just as a game never reaches true finality; the game can always be played again and again and players will always be drawn into its horizon.

What Gadamer also wants to emphasize with the notion of play is how art is more than the heightened state of feeling or **aesthetic consciousness** emphasised by much post-Kantian aesthetics. We need to take account of two relationships at work in the operation of play. On the one hand, there is the dynamic between the players and the game, on the other there is the relationship between the players and the spectators, what Gadamer's terms a 'playing along with'. Concerning the players and the game, the game always takes precedence over the individual players. Sure enough, teams will always have their star players and key individuals who gain glory for personal achievements, but the team, and more importantly the game itself wherein the play is enacted, will always be more extensive than the actions of the players.

This is a direct comment on the limitations of **subjectivity**. Gadamer draws an analogy between forms of understanding and the individual. In subsuming the individual players to the greater structure of the team or the game itself, Gadamer echoes the attack on **subjectivity** where individual reflection is a fragment of larger hermeneutical structures ('the closed circuits of historical life'), those of language and tradition.

All art and artistry in some way draws upon play. Mention has already been made of the obvious play of a team game. In a drama presentation, that is, a 'play', the audience is essential to the performance in the same way as spectators make a necessary contribution to a football match; for example, the spectators contribute something to the character of the game.

Gadamer also refers to dancing, pointing out that the German word for play, *Spiel*, originally meant 'dance' (**TM**, p. 103). Dancing seems to be a clear illustration of the to-and-fro play already mentioned: a patterned activity, which yet remains unpredictable as to development and eventual outcome. Music is also a form of play, the most obvious sense of which is captured in the everyday expression 'to *play* a musical instrument'.

The playfulness of the visual arts is perhaps less obvious and rather more difficult to grasp in the first instance, but on reflection a plausible explanation is something along these lines. A painting draws the viewer into the world of the picture and the interaction with the viewer is playful in the sense that there is a to-and-fro dynamic between artwork and viewer. One speaks of the way the work of art offers the viewer a world, a horizon of meaning; this we saw in relation to Heidegger. The painting invites and draws the viewer into its own world and the viewer is engaged in a constant activity of interrogating that world. The meaning of the painting is never fully disclosed as it is always the world of the painting as it engages in dialogue with the world of the viewer. As we can see, the artwork operates in Gadamer's view as just another partner in a hermeneutical dialogue. Just as truth is essentially dialogue, so too is art and its truth.

The poetic word By means of the poetic word, Gadamer says, 'language emerges in its full autonomy ... language just stands for itself: it brings itself to stand before us' (Hahn, 1997, p. 39). Whereas 'ordinary language resembles a coin that we pass round among ourselves in place of something else', he claims, 'poetic language is like gold itself' (Gadamer, 1986b, p. 67).

Those who find Gadamer's style imprecise will no doubt find the 'poetic language' term infuriatingly vague. So what does it mean? The later essays are scattered with helpful clues. It is evidently not limited to the language of poetry although poetry, especially modern, hermetic lyric poetry, is the most 'poetic' of 'poetic language'. Gadamer constructs a kind of hierarchy of the poetic, 'ascending from lyric poetry through epic and tragedy ... leading to the novel and any demanding prose' (Gadamer, 1986b, p. 136). We are not simply being directed towards 'literary' uses of language but degrees of translatability. The language of the novel, being close to the structures of everyday speech, is the least problematic; the lyric poem flatly resists translation. 'No translation of a lyric poem ever conveys the original work,' he says, 'the best we can hope for is that one poet should come across another and put a new poetic work, as it were, in place of the original by creating an equivalent with the materials of a different language' (Gadamer, 1986b, p. 111). Gadamer speaks of 'eminence'. Here 'poetic compositions are text in a new kind of sense: they are text in an eminent sense of the word ... In this kind of text language emerges in its full autonomy. Here language just stands for itself: it brings itself to stand before us' (Hahn, 1997, p. 39). The poetic word is e-minent, it protrudes, juts out, in the literal sense, it refuses to be consumed or 'used up', as Heidegger says, in his essay **The Origin of the Work of Art**. In ordinary language words disappear into their function, they vanish in the face of the matters at issue. In poetic language words take on a life of their own, in this sense. In ordinary language, the language of 'the homeland', we are more attentive to the message rather than the medium, but with the poetic, the word's 'corporeality' shines forth. Words in their embodiment, their sounds, modulation, tonality, tempo, dynamics, extraneous factors in the exchange of information of everyday speech, come to life in the poetic utterance. Those who hear the words also come to life. The poetic word, in passing beyond mere information, disrupts the everyday (and our situatedness within it). Gadamer here refers us to the hermeneutical 'experience of being pulled up short' (**TM**, p. 268), an experience we undergo when reading a text. We are suddenly alienated from the text as it thwarts our expectations through its novelty.

In ordinary language there is invariably an element of inventiveness present. The operation of the '**hermeneutic circle**' demonstrates this and shows how meaning is never static, unitary or foreclosed. This inventive, self-transformative quality is heightened and intensified in the poetic utterance. In lyric poetry particularly, 'the poet releases the multidimensionality of the associations of meaning which is suppressed by practical unity of intention in logically controlled, one-dimensional everyday speech' (Gadamer, 1997, p. 167). As if to demonstrate the truth of his claim Gadamer, in his essay Who am I and Who are you? a reading of **Paul Celan**'s 'Breath turn' (Atemwende) or 'Breathcrystal' (Atemkristall), analyses the ways the readers sense of individuation and identity are disturbed and unsettled by these verses.

The whole question of who is addressing whom in the decontextualised zone of the poetic, raises important questions for Gadamer. Meaning is ultimately a dialogue, a negotiation. 'In a poem', Gadamer says, 'with whom does ... communication take place? Is it with the reader? With which *reader*? Here the dialectic of question and answer which is always the basis of the hermeneutic process, and which corresponds to the basic structure of the dialogue, undergoes a special modification'. (Hahn, 1997, pp. 39–40). Quite what this special modification is he does not spell out but he says a little later in this essay something worthy of note.

> 'As I look back today I see one point in particular where I did not achieve the theoretical consistency I strove for in ***Truth and Method***. I did not make it clear enough how the ... basic projects that were brought together in the concept of *play* harmonized. ... On the one hand there is the orientation to the game we play with art and on the other the grounding of language in conversation, the game of language ... I needed to unite the game of language more closely with the game art plays' (See **eminent text**).

Positivism   Positivism, in its most general form, refers to the foundations of knowledge; it affirms the belief, like empiricism, that all knowledge is ultimately based upon sense-experience. Genuine knowledge is nothing more than the description and explanation of empirical facts. (See the **positivism dispute**.)

Positivism dispute   In the 1960s in Germany there was a debate about the role of positivism in the social sciences. Against the positivistic view that the social sciences were objective and value–free were the critical theorists **Jürgen Habermas** and **Theodor Adorno**. Although Habermas was ultimately critical of Gadamer's **philosophical hermeneutics**, which he took to be conservative and uncritical of the role of ideology in the production of knowledge, he utilized hermeneutics as a defence against the claims of positivistic social science.

Postmodernism   Postmodernism is one of those terms that defy easy definition as there are so many versions of what it actually is. In one sense it is part of a body of opinion that rejects modernism; and philosophical modernism is just another way of expressing the 'Enlightenment project', as the period of the **Enlightenment** and the early modern age are roughly parallel. Postmodernism, whose hero is generally taken to be **Friedrich**

Nietzsche, is an ironic, playful and sceptical response to modernism. Modernism, with its trust in the power of progress through reason and its allegiance to universal ethical and epistemological standards, is mocked by postmodernism. To be post-modern is to be sceptical or ironic about knowledge's absolute grounding in reason or the self-authenticating subject. It is very difficult to locate Gadamer within the modern/post-modern opposition. In one sense he is clearly post-modern in his critical attitude to the 'Enlightenment project' and the assumption within **philosophical hermeneutics** that knowledge is historical and ungrounded. On the other hand Gadamer does not seek to move beyond modernism; if anything his work seeks to reclaim and re-evaluate the pre-modern. In reviving notions of **authority** and **tradition** he, at the same time, rejects the idea of a radical rupture between the ancient or classical, the modern, and the post-modern.

Practice *(praxis)*   Gadamer finds in the Aristotelian concepts of *praxis* and *phronesis* a space for ethical thinking that is independent with respect to theory and technique, but also to a general metaphysics. According to Gadamer, it is to Aristotle's great merit to have refused the path of Platonic idealism, asserting that the good is always locatable in various concrete actions. In light of this, Gadamer takes over the Aristotelian distinction between *praxis* and *poiesis*, that is, between moral-practical knowledge and practical-technical knowledge. Taken together, both fields of knowledge motivate or drive action, with the important difference that the latter is applied in accordance with established models, while the former, which determines correct moral action, is a synthesis between ends and means that needs deliberate judgment about an individual course of action in a given situation.

In order to illustrate the mediation between universal and particular, Gadamer refers to Aristotle's ethics and in particular the concept of practical knowing. It is in this Aristotelian concept that Gadamer finds his own solution to the dilemma of ethical practice, namely the relationship between the universality of law, which meets the needs of absolute and unconditional obligation, and the variability and multiplicity of concrete lived situations, which express the historicity of the human condition. *Phronesis*, an intellectual virtue, is an example of a form of knowledge that is also hermeneutic, one that is not pure or disinterested (it is not 'objective' in the scientific sense of the term), since the deliberation and application constitute essential moments in practical knowledge. Hence *phronesis* is not a logical-deductive application of a universal truth to a particular case; it is rather a historical mediation of a universal need and a particular situation. In a word, the right course of action is never determined independently of the situation in which I must act correctly. According to Gadamer, by interpreting moral judgments as a synthesis of *logos* and *ethos*, Aristotle was able to remove from moral knowing the pretence of unconditional supra-historical objectivity by drawing attention to the historical dimension of human knowledge, a dimension that remains a fundamental concern for hermeneutics.

Prejudice   Prejudice is in some ways the most important of the trinity of prejudice, tradition and authority, as Gadamer's treatment of it tells us much about his philosophical procedures and commitments. Like **tradition** and **authority**, prejudice has suffered distortion at the hands of the enlightenment: 'There is one prejudice of the Enlightenment that defines its essence: the fundamental prejudice of the Enlightenment is the prejudice against prejudice itself' (*TM*, p. 270). Like **authority**, there is both a positive and negative reading of the term prejudice, and the enlightenment emphasized the negative while neglecting the positive. Gadamer seeks to uncover and retrieve submerged meanings of terms encrusted with the prejudices of modernity.

The word 'prejudice' etymologically breaks down into *pre-judice* or pre-judgement. Judgement is not possible without the 'pre' that comes before it. All judgements are conditioned by prejudgements. This is an older, pre-modern sense of prejudice to which Gadamer wants to draw our attention, whereas the familiar understanding of prejudice is unreflective judgement or over-hasty reasoning, resulting in the bigotry of purely subjective opinion or the unreflective parroting of purely received wisdom. The point being made here is that judgements are made possible not by an abstract and neutral reason but a set of pre-reflective involvements with the world that stand behind judgements and in fact make them possible. A condition of making reflective and evaluative judgements about the world is the possession of prejudices: without prejudgements there can be no judgements. (Also see **understanding**.)

Pre-Socratic philosophers   The group of philosophers who pre-date Socrates. They are the earliest of the recorded Greek thinkers and are notable for their attempts to discover the fundamental nature of being. Gadamer produced two studies on the two principal philosophers of this group. In *The Beginning of Philosophy* he concentrates on **Parmenides** and in *The Beginning of Knowledge* the focus is upon **Heraclitus**. (See *The Beginning of Philosophy* and *The Beginning of Knowledge*.)

The principle of charity   In rhetoric and hermeneutics, the principle of charity assumes that when something is written or uttered it is reasonable to ascribe meaning to it, to assume that it makes some sense. The principle is charitable because the interpreter is constantly reaching out in search of agreement, constantly seeking to make sense of what is being said. Without the principle of charity it would be all too easy wilfully to misunderstand what the other is saying and cause communication to break down. Gadamer's philosophical hermeneutics would appear to assume the correctness of the **principle of charity**. (See the **hermeneutics of trust** and the **hermeneutics of suspicion**.)

Principle   of   effective   history (See 'historically   effected consciousness' and 'effective historical consciousness'.)

Problem history   A way of studying the history of philosophy that takes all past philosophical systems to be no more than solutions or approaches to a stock of timeless and enduring philosophical problems. For this version of the history of philosophy, popularized by neo-Kantians at the end of the nineteenth century, there is no real development in philosophy, for although systems may change the perennial problems do not.

—R—

Rationality   The traditional philosophical account of reason, in the modern period, refers to a mode of thought that makes universal claims about what it is reasonable to think or do. The claim here is that certain assertions can be made, and conclusions determined, regardless of historical or social circumstances, because they appeal to something more overarching and less parochial. For example, the notion of a 'general will' assumes a form of thought that has general applicability on the basis of a uniform and common rationality. Against this notion of universalizable reason is the idea that rationality is more localized and historically mediated. Following in the footsteps of **Hegel**, Gadamer embeds reason within a specifically historical location and rejects the grander modernist conception of an unencumbered rationality.

***Reason in the Age of Science* (1976)**   A collection of eight essays by Gadamer exploring the following themes: the relationship between philosophy and science; the nature of reason; and the idea of hermeneutics as a practical activity.

Relativism   Relativism is a philosophical thesis with many forms; it can be variously historical, cultural, conceptual and epistemological. In every version the claim is that there is no absolute truth outside truths that are embedded within cultures and historical processes, and hence truth is a relative term. This means that there is no gold standard of truth, as it were: all systems are judged by their own standards of internal consistency or whatever, but not by some externally valid criterion. **Philosophical hermeneutics** is often taken to be relativistic because it takes human understanding, like truth, to be without finality and completion, and hence historically relativist.

The Relevance of the Beautiful and other essays   The title essay was first published in 1977 and the other essays in this collection were published in 1967 and 1977. This work is made up of an extended essay entitled 'The Relevance of the Beautiful' and a collection of shorter essays. The dominant theme in all these works is the philosophy of art or aesthetics. Art is a central theme in Gadamer's main work ***Truth and Method***, but there it features as an aspect of the more central concern of truth, and the nature of art itself is not explored in any detail. In 'The Relevance of the Beautiful' a more detailed and extended treatment of art, in the broadest sense of the word, is offered. The subtitle of the essay is 'Art as play, symbol and festival' and these three themes are explored in detail in the major essay and the shorter works in the collection.

Two other aspects of art, symbol and festival, supplement play in the essay 'The relevance of the beautiful'. Symbol is understood initially in its Greek original. In the ancient world a symbol was one piece of a broken object given to a guest. The other matching piece was kept by the provider of hospitality in the hope that if the two met in future 'the two pieces could be fitted together again to form a whole in an act of recognition,' and consequently, 'the symbol represented something like a sort of pass used in the ancient world: something in and through which we recognize something already known to us' (Gadamer, 1986b, p. 31). In some rather obscure way the relationship between the possessors of the broken object is replicated in the connection between the artwork and the perceiver. Another example Gadamer gives from the classical world comes from Plato's *Symposium* where Aristophanes, the playwright, tells us that, '(O)riginally all human beings were spherical creatures. But later on, on account of their misbehaviour, the gods cut them in two. Thereafter, each of the halves, which originally belonged to one complete living being, seeks to be made whole once again. Thus every individual is a fragment . . .'. Gadamer is rather elusive on the full applicability of these analogies to his sense of 'symbol' but his meaning seems to be something along these lines. The meaning of the artwork is not conditioned by or reducible to a story about its historical placing or its positioning within a specific artistic genre. The meaning of the artwork is inscrutable and not immediately apparent; nevertheless, we turn to the work of art, in our search for the significance of our own lives, as if the work of art is going to complete the puzzle of existence in the way that the matching objects link together in an act of recognition as in the first illustration. What Gadamer seems to be getting at is that the artwork, although symbolic, does not represent something else, or stand for a hidden meaning that needs to be accessed or explained. The artwork displays itself, but as symbol it is a vehicle for attempted acts of self-recognition. We seek to understand ourselves in the artwork; this is why art captivates and intrigues, drawing us into its world, however seemingly remote and distant that world at first appears. Gadamer warns against using the artwork as symbolic in the sense of having a hidden code that we must crack in order to make sense of the work's hidden 'message'. On the contrary, what you see is what you get, the artwork says what it says through what it discloses, but this is always something more than the perceiver can take account of and acknowledge. The meaning of the artwork is never complete as we will always be able to recognize new things within it. The artwork reveals aspects of a human world and its limitations just as much as we reveal aspects of the world of the artwork (and its imitations) in an uneasy – because constantly changing – totality. The true *being* of the work of art will never be fully grasped; there will always be an aura of uniqueness and irreplaceability surrounding works of art. Gadamer also speaks of artwork as festive in the sense of being bound up with the celebration and remembering of festivals. If the notion of 'symbol' points to the being of the work of art, the notion of festival is more obviously aimed at revealing its temporality, its relationship to the time of its reception and the notion of time the festival demonstrates. In the essay 'The festive character of theatre', Gadamer asks about the meaning of festivals and gives the following response:

> 'Festivals are to be celebrated. But what is the festive character
> of a festival? Naturally, this quality need not always be associ-
> ated with joy or happiness, since in mourning we also share
> this festive character together. But a festive occasion is always
> something uplifting which raises the participants out of their
> everyday existence and elevates them into a kind of universal
> communion' (Gadamer, 1986, p. 58).

The raising up and out of everyday existence is obviously something the participants experience and it is made possible through the festival's appro-priation of its own temporality; it has the effect of suspending the everyday experience of time and this has the effect of injecting a note of mystery to the festival. Gadamer illustrates his point by referring to the festival of Christmas. Here is a festival that celebrates an event that happened more than two thousand years ago and yet it happens every year, and even so every Christmas celebration is different. The festival creates its own time which bursts through the mundane clock time of the diurnal and the everyday. Art is festive in the sense that it too disrupts and dislocates our everyday experience of time; it lifts us out of our daily routines and offers the opportunity to imagine ourselves and our engagements with the world differently. Gadamer says, 'It is of the nature of the festival that it should proffer time, arresting it and allowing it to tarry. That is what festive celebration means. The calculating way in which we normally manage and dispose of time is, as it were, brought to a standstill' (Gadamer, 1986, p. 42).

As the example of mourning testifies, the festival is also an act of sharing. The festival binds and brings together the community in more intimate and important ways than other experiences of solidarity and togetherness. The community need not be localized and parochial. Gadamer gives the example of witnessing Greek antiquities in the National Museum of Athens. He speaks of being 'overcome by an all-embracing festive quiet' and notes that one 'senses how everyone is gathered together for something' (Gadamer, 1986b, p. 40). In marvelling at ancient Greek artefacts, one is experiencing the sense in which all participants are part of a common historical and cultural heritage. The notion of tradition is important again here. Gadamer suggests that great art binds in so far as we experience ourselves as a larger whole, a part of western culture and a part of a common humanity.

Art is truthful because it, like other forms of dialogue, 'says something to someone'. But because the experience of art is the experience of meaning, it demonstrates that art is ultimately subordinate to, because part of, hermeneutics. Gadamer says, 'Aesthetics must be swallowed up in hermeneutics'.

Rhetoric   From Heidegger, Gadamer took over and radicalized the idea of the historicity of mankind as a destiny, and gave it a more concrete sense, with the revaluation of **prejudice** and **tradition** as moments determining the **hermeneutic circle**. With the recovery of the humanist tradition, specifically Giovanni Battista Vico's account of rhetoric and the idea of practical wisdom, and especially the idea of practical wisdom, he defined a concept of history that is neither objective nor subjective. This is opposed not only to the possibility of general laws that explain history, but also to historical hermeneutics understood as objective science.

Gadamer's interest in rhetoric belongs to his overall re-evaluation of language as it pertains to the belonging together of human beings within a socio-linguistic world. With the rehabilitation of the much maligned concept of rhetoric in modernity, Gadamer is trying to call into question an understanding of language that reduces it to a mere tool of rational exchange and communication. In his attempt to broaden the concept of language, Gadamer argues – against the anti-rhetorical bent of modernity – that rhetoric should not simply be understood in terms of sophistic persuasion or affective delivery, but rather in terms of speaking well in the dialectical sense, i.e. the cultivation 'of arguments that are convincing' and not simply 'logically compelling' (*TM*, p. 571). The rhetorical space of reasoning that Gadamer refers to here belongs to human practice and rational deliberation, and not simply to the space of feelings and affections. As Gadamer puts it: 'I find it frighteningly unreal when people like Habermas ascribe to rhetoric a compulsory quality that one must reject in favour of unconstrained, rational dialogue. This is to underestimate not only the danger of the glib manipulation and incapacitation of reason but also the possibility of coming to an understanding through persuasion, on which social life depends' (*TM*, p. 571).

After the publication of **Truth and Method**, Gadamer admitted that the relationship between rhetoric and hermeneutics, the relationship between rhetoric and dialectic, still needed to be worked out more fully, but felt that there was a genuine reciprocal relationship between the two. As already shown in **Truth and Method**, hermeneutics shares with rhetoric the possible delimitation of theoretical truth and practical knowing, which means that the latter field is founded on the demonstrative persuasiveness of convincing arguments or believable statements which are not simply logically valid or conclusive proofs. Drawing on Plato and Aristotle, Gadamer argues that rhetoric finds its rightful place when we accept that knowledge is not reducible to theoretical knowing and that we cannot expect the same level of precision in the different fields of knowledge. Again, it should not be forgotten that Gadamer is drawing heavily upon Plato's and Aristotle's account of the soul and the proper care for the soul, insofar as good rhetoric allows the right kinds of words to exercise an effect on the educated soul in the right way. Thus, against the extreme overestimation of reason's authority in modernity, Gadamer is trying to question the dominant universalistic pretensions of scientific rationalism. He does this by defending and defining a more nuanced account of rhetoric from which it is possible to delimit its scope within a shared linguistic *polis* and against the horizon of our always having to act responsibly without knowing all the consequences of our actions. In short, Gadamer's defence and rehabilitation of rhetoric seems to broaden the universality of understanding and this process takes place within the field of intersubjective commonality.

Ricoeur, Paul (1913–2005) French philosopher whose pioneering work on hermeneutics, under the inspiration of Husserl, Heidegger, Karl Jaspers and Gabriel Marcel, was hugely influential on contemporary continental philosophy, and his multifaceted work stands, along with Gadamer's, as the most important contemporary development of hermeneutics. The complexity of what Ricoeur called the 'long route' via hermeneutic detours, specifically in relation to what he considered Heidegger's 'short route' through existential-ontological hermeneutics, could be summarized in the following way: the Cogito is in being and not the other way round, an insight which constitutes a new form of Copernican revolution for philosophy in that, unlike all modern philosophy inspired by the Cogito, being that emerges from the Cogito still has to discover that it is in fact the Cogito which emerges and expresses itself as being in the world. In a word, Ricoeur tries to bring the Cartesian Cogito back into the opaque depth of human existence, challenging its self-transparency and calling into question whether or not it is simply the seat of conscious conceptual operations. Hermeneutics thus becomes the critical interpretation which aims to dislodge the Cogito from its presumed clarity and distinctness and to engage it in the dramatic adventure of human existence.

Unlike Gadamer, Ricoeur's interest in Freudian psychoanalysis is of particular significance, insofar as psychoanalysis attempts to identify the demystification of consciousness and the philosophy of the Cogito that strives for clarity and distinctness. In addition, psychoanalysis recognizes that there is desire as submerged desire, an unconscious desire that seeks to make itself manifest, and existence is revealed primarily in terms of an archaeology of subjectivity and its driving motivation. However, unlike Freud, Ricoeur believes that the human being is not only its unconscious striving, but is also bound up with a universe that is ontologically relational and involves the active self and its shared world. Thus Ricoeur's hermeneutics is forced to move from an attitude that is purely phenomenological, and hence both descriptive and eidetic, to an attitude which is truly hermeneutical, one which links symbols to the richness of lived interpretation and experienced meaning.

Heidegger's phenomenological hermeneutics is reflected in Ricoeur's hermeneutics of the symbol, insofar as both thinkers, their notable differences notwithstanding, developed a way of thinking that attempted to understand how and who man really is and to acknowledge the finitude at the heart of human understanding. Unlike Heidegger, however, Ricoeur never broke fully with Husserlian phenomenology or with a post-Cartesian philosophy of reflection, considering both positions complementary paths in the journey of a hermeneutics of the symbol. Reflection and interpretation are in fact complementary for Ricoeur, two moments of a process of inter-pretation that integrate the Cogito with the knowledge that the concrete human situation is not one rooted at the centre of existence, but also divided against oneself, lost in the world and separated from others. Freud's discovery of the unconscious takes on precisely this meaning. But Ricoeur's hermeneutics of the symbol is not only regressive, it does not serve the archaic path alone, but, due to the overabundance of symbols, it must also be critically demystifying and restorative. Hence Ricoeur's hermeneutics interprets consciousness through its symbols, it learns how to return to parts of the past, but also how to open the present up to the future, and to philosophical renewal as such. This, according to Ricoeur, is the ethical significance of hermeneutics.

Ricoeur's hermeneutics of the long route reaches an interpretation of man's being in truth that moves along the path of symbolic interpre-tation and meaningful expression. Thus, Ricoeur attempts to mediate between what we might call transcendental and eidetic phenomenology and Heidegger's ontological hermeneutics that attempts to index philo-sophical understanding to the historical situatedness of the interpreter. For Ricoeur, however, Heidegger's so-called ontological-hermeneutical 'short route' does not stay with the discussion of method but leaps ahead to the question of ontological meaning, which is founded on understanding, not as a way of knowing, but as a way of being. The methodological aspect of hermeneutics, just like the transcendental and eidetic dimension of phenomenology, is hugely significant for Ricoeur, and he thus brings to bear both examples from analytic philosophy of language and from epistemology. However, Ricoeur is not attempting to undermine the ontological herme-neutics of Heidegger, but rather intends to enrich it – via the 'long route' – with the contributions that can come from all those disciplines engaged in the interpretation based on methodological criteria. This concern with methodology is what marks Ricoeur off from Heidegger. For this reason, against Gadamer's opposition between 'hermeneutic truth' and 'method', Ricoeur does not see them as antithetical but rather complementary, always seeking a path of philosophy in dialogue with the sciences, with the different methods of interpretation for a synthesis between ontological hermeneutics, transcendental hermeneutics and hermeneutic methodology. Ricoeur's hermeneutic method is not a hermeneutics of symbols over and against ontological meaning, but wants to establish itself as a more radical way of analyzing a hermeneutics of ontological meaning. Albeit differently from Gadamer, the **hermeneutic circle** is nevertheless a constant principle of his **philosophical hermeneutics**, and is perhaps better defined as a true logical hermeneutics. Ricoeur, in his *Logique hermenéutique*, explicitly locates a 'logical hermeneutics' operative within the **hermeneutic circle**. This is a hermeneutical logic, he tells us, which does not, in principle, oppose itself to classical logic, but rather attempts to sketch the limits of the interpretation and understanding of historical and spiritual human products, formulating the principle that everything must be encompassed by the process of interpretation and understanding.

For Gadamer and Ricoeur, then, the very being that Heidegger believed to be the preparatory condition for existential-hermeneutical analysis, namely *Dasein*, must encompass the identification of practical everyday ways of being in which the processes of historical transmission take place in inter-pretation and understanding. Thus both philosophers argue that through the ontological horizon of *Dasein*, Heidegger is in fact defining the contours of the horizon of pre-understanding that accompanies every process of interpretation. At the same time, however, they are also establishing more clearly than Heidegger that the otherness of any objective historical reality must be interpreted from the perspective of everydayness. In other words, the **hermeneutic circle** is specified as the particular relationship established between an interpreter, aware of moving and being moved within their own pre-conceived or prejudiced horizon, yet willing to understand the object of experience and understanding in its otherness and in its historical truth. Thus the logic of the **hermeneutic circle** is the awareness of the requirements of its pre-conceived horizon, the constant attempt to interpret and understand the truth in its otherness, which means first and foremost that a recognition of otherness must be accomplished and that this model of recognition is not arbitrarily subsuming this otherness under the same. The **hermeneutic circle**, then, far from representing the logical fallacy of constitutive hermeneutics, attempts to make it truthful.

Like Gadamer, Ricoeur also tries to overcome the excessive hubris of rationalism, which fails to recognize the much-neglected role of pre-under-standing. Hermeneutics thus proceeds from the same pre-understanding of what it aims to understand and this form of thinking has the critical task of recovering all those dimensions of marginalized thought, namely symbol, myth and the sacred, which modern philosophy has arguably expunged from the horizon of truth. Ricoeur shows, once again, how it is possible to combine the logic of the **hermeneutic circle** with transcendental-ontological hermeneutics. Whether Gadamer operates with a similar transcendental-ontological hermeneutic position is highly dubious, insofar as Gadamer is attempting to inhabit a space 'between' phenomenology and dialectic, 'between' pure language and pure insight, 'between' dialectic and intuition, 'between' word and concept, and 'between' realism and **idealism**.

Romantic Hermeneutics developed Romantic Hermeneutics as a technique that could deepen the psychological understanding of a text by arguing that the interpreter of a text should not be completely bound to the text or the authorial intention behind the text, but should rather take a certain distance from the text and in doing so develop an interpretative autonomy and freedom. Ultimately, according to Romantic Hermeneutics, it is possible to understand a text better than the author himself. In addition, Romantic Hermeneutics possessed a distinct awareness of historical distance that separates modernity from the classical tradition. This awareness emphasized that the strangeness and seemingly insurmountable force of **tradition** needs to be overcome by means of a productive access to the past, and it is in the concept of historical research that it will find a critical category capable of mediating between past and present. For Schleiermacher, then, the interpreter understands the text only when he/she brings to light an awareness of the meaning of the author's intention. Schleiermacher's **hermeneutics** shows its romantic predilection in attempting to trace the subjectivity or subjective intent of the author, insofar as language is not taken as a mere grammatical object, but rather as the dimension through which one can trace the living thought of the author. The ultimate goal of Schleiermacher's hermeneutic theory is not so much the interpretation of the text as the interpretation of the author's often hidden intentions. The interpretation of the author should allow the reader to understand a text better than it was understood by the writer himself.

In the Romantic period, hermeneutics extends its investigation well beyond the confines of a hermeneutics of sacred texts: the problem of understanding no longer applies only to written texts, but to any linguistic-communicative relationship, including interpersonal communication, and the Platonic dialogue, which is structured in terms of question and answer, becomes the model of understanding. For Schleiermacher, the problem of interpretation comes to the fore when misunderstandings arise. The arrangement of **language** in a work and the work of a single author are insufficient to understand the universality of the language, the person or cultural context: the two considerations should throw light on each other and this is the interpretation of Schleiermacher's **hermeneutic circle**. His work also offers itself as a reconstructive hermeneutics: the technique of authorial mastery, as opposed to focusing on artistic creativity and authorial motivation. Instead, the interpreter, who provides a broader and richer context, understands the author better than the author himself. The interpreter can then reconstruct the genesis of the work through two different moments of interpretation, a grammatical one, i.e. the linguistic aspects of the text, and a creative psychological moment that concerns artistic institution as an expression of a particular form of life.

The experience of interpretative estrangement and the possibility of misunderstanding are not accidental happenings; however, the general concerns present in any meaningful discourse remain somewhat shrouded in mystery, since the other is always obscured to some extent. Therefore, interpretation is not a mere crutch for understanding, but is necessary for the realization or actualization of it. Hence misunderstanding occurs spontaneously, and understanding must remain optimal and sought after. Schleiermacher also makes a radical shift in perspective: what is to be interpreted is not the text, its objective meaning, but the identity of the one who speaks and writes; hermeneutics becomes an art which has the task of understanding and interpreting, be it written or oral, another person. Individuality is the origin of language, which, in its concrete knowability, represents a synthesis between two linguistic dimensions: the universal – the common language which includes speakers who make communication possible – and the individual, that continually innovative element, which is the expression of a unique world-view.

Romantic Hermeneutics thus includes an analysis of grammatical and psychological interpretation, and defines them separately yet acknowledges their co-belonging in understanding. Grammar is the interpretation which focuses on the individual ambit and historical language via the cultural context in which the author lived. The interpretation is psychological, however, when it aims at the individual writer or speaker and his/her need to communicate inwardness, to grasp the specific meaning of the original words. Schleiermacher thus shows that hermeneutics always presupposes the operative nature of language. Yet this is only the expression of thought, the exteriorization of interiority: the speech act is always bound up with a broader linguistic horizon which the author expresses and which he is to be understood against – a common horizon – while at the same time creatively expressing his own historical individuality. Therefore both the psychological and grammatical interpretations have as their tasks the grasping of what is common to, and given in, language. According to the psychological approach, the object of interpretation is a subjective act, a creative act of aesthetic form or artistic thought. Consequently, hermeneutics cannot devote itself to rule establishment or rule following, but must rather reveal an individuality that embodies a creative necessity. Therefore interpreting a text is to repeat the act of its creator, to get to the level of the author, which for Schleiermacher means understanding an author better than he understands himself. Gadamer's critical response to Romantic Hermeneutics is best summed up in **Truth and Method** when he writes: '... what constitutes the hermeneutical event proper is not language as language, whether as grammar or as lexicon; it consists in the coming into language of what has been said in the tradition: an event that is at once appropriation and interpretation. Thus here it really is true to say that this event is not our action upon the thing, but the act of the thing itself' (**TM** p. 459).

Rorty, Richard (1931–2007) Richard Rorty, an American philosopher working within the tradition of pragmatism, is a key figure in the development of contemporary philosophy. His ground breaking *Philosophy and the Mirror of Nature* introduced the work of Gadamer to many in the English-speaking world. In this work Rorty argued that philosophy, since the seventeenth century, was dominated by a single conception of the mind. The mind was taken to be a 'mirror of nature', that is, a means whereby the world as it really is gets accurately represented. For Rorty, the theme of representation, the power of the human mind to mirror reality, explains the centrality of epistemology in many of the strands of philosophical thought over the last three hundred years or so. But Rorty seeks to show that within a larger historical framework this theme of representation is both relatively recent and, importantly, little more than a controlling metaphor for talking about the mind. In other words, representation does not give direct access to truth; it is no more than a particular perspective. Philosophy needs to drop the idea of a royal road to truth and look for alternative metaphors for understanding the world. In the interests of breaking new ground he suggests that Gadamer's **hermeneutics**, with its emphasis upon the power of dialogue and conversation to open up new lines of thought, offers a potentially fruitful alternative to representation: more fallible, but potentially more illuminating. In the final chapter of *Philosophy and the Mirror of Nature*, entitled 'Philosophy without mirrors', Rorty rejects the idea of philosophy as the pursuit of truth (through representation). He prefers to speak instead of *Bildung* or 'edification'; philosophy does not grant truth but through a plurality of conversations, of which philosophy is only one voice, we might achieve some measure of edification. Rorty directly attributes these ideas to Gadamer.

Rorty was present at the celebrations to honour Gadamer's one-hundredth birthday and the address he gave is a very good introduction to his appropriation of Gadamer's work (See Rorty 2000).

— S —

Schleiermacher, F. D. E. (1768–1834) Schleiermacher was the founding father of modern classical hermeneutics and the first to offer a hermeneutic philosophy that claimed to be rigorously scientific and systematically universalizable. Schleiermacher's thought was influenced by at least five historico-philosophical elements: the teachings of pietism; a deep knowledge of and abiding interest in the ancients, in particular, Plato; the influence of the early Romantics, cf. his friendship with Friedrich Schlegel (1772–1829); and a lasting confrontation with Kant's moral philosophy and Fichte's critical idealism. The main focus of Schleiermacher's interests is the philosophy of religion and theology. In contrast with the cold rationalism of the Enlightenment, Schleiermacher defines religion as a lived intuition of universality as infinite in the form of feeling. Or as Gadamer puts it: 'Everything finite [for Schleiermacher] is an expression, a representation of the infinite' (*TM* p. 55). To say that religion is an intuition of universality simply implies the feeling of a dependency of the finite on the infinite, of man's dependency on God, which for Schleiermacher is the very definition of an authentically religious attitude. This explains the fact that religion has historically assumed various forms and has been institutionalized in a plurality of faiths. Schleiermacher not only concentrates his philosophical reflections on religious issues, but also on issues such as philosophical dialectic and ethics. Human knowledge is trapped between two antithetical poles: on one hand, we have empirical reality, i.e. nature, and on the other, we have the form of thought, ideality and the rational element. However, according to Schleiermacher, the finite human being is incapable of drawing these two poles together since conceptual knowledge necessarily takes its start from oppositions and distinctions, and hence these poles must remain poles apart.

In terms of Schleiermacher's contributions to hermeneutics, one cannot look past his attempt, inspired by Schlegel, to establish a method of concrete exegetical analysis that would lead to an interpretative understanding of the internal form of a work, its relation to the author and to the totality of his/her production. The steps involved in this hermeneutical endeavour are 1) an attention to the context: striking a balance between historico-psychological interpretation and grammatical/philological interpretation; and 2) an emphasis on the fact that hermeneutics must aspire to be a rigorous science concerned with the object of interpretation which is historically remote, potentially obscure and complex. With these steps, Schleiermacher understands interpretation as a scientific, penetrating and creative reconstruction of a work assessed from within the lived, psychological perspective of the author. This amounts, according to Gadamer, to 're-establishing the "world" to which it [the work] belongs' (*TM*, p. 159). Hence hermeneutics as a restorative enterprise is an artful attempt that has as its task the understanding and interpretation of a historical conversation, be it oral or written, of another person and the original particularity of their authorial intent and situation.

Schleiermacher realized that the science of hermeneutics is bound up tightly with language and that it presupposes language as its very condition. Yet language, for Schleiermacher, is always an expression of thought which helps us to exteriorize our interiority. Every linguistic act is creative, yet at the same time it is tied to the specific language through which the author expresses him or herself. Thus language represents something communal through which we can express our individual interiority. Schleiermacher's emphasis on grammatical interpretation tries to gather together the commonality of every exterior linguistic expression, while his psychological interpretation dwells on the ineluctable individuality (e.g. an author's unique ways of thinking, feeling and reasoning) which is ever present in written and oral conversation. However, Schleiermacher's hermeneutic method is not solely an attempt to enter interpretatively into the intentional life of the author, to understand the author as the author understood himself or herself, but rather to understand the author better than they understood themselves (*Besserverstehen*). What Schleiermacher is after is an understanding of authorial intention and creativity from within the process of the work's 'inner origin', a process that remains for the most part hidden from the author.

What Schleiermacher also establishes is a second hermeneutical principle: one can gain access to the matter in question through the principle of intuition (*Einfühlung*), which indicates going beyond the external rules and canons of methodological hermeneutics, characterized as a process of identification with the interiority of the author. To understand a text truly, one should be able to understand all the cultural, poetic, religious, literary and spiritual concerns which presided over its creation through a process of empathy and intuition. All this is done from the perspective of the author's own intentions, so that one can relive, and understand better, all the inner spiritual processes which led to the work's creation and the expressiveness of its language.

The main bone of contention that Gadamer has with Schleiermacher's brand of universal hermeneutics is with its claim that interpretative understanding is an 'understanding better' in terms of reproductive repetition of authorial intent. Against this ambitious claim, Gadamer offers something altogether different: all understanding is an understanding differently or 'that we understand in a *different way, if we understand at all*' (*TM*, p. 296). Due to Gadamer's Heideggerian heritage, and the ontological turn that his hermeneutics took, he submits that any attempted reconstruction of an original text is essentially a futile enterprise owing to the historicity of our being. However, it is precisely in Gadamer's appropriation of the **hermeneutic circle** from Heidegger, and Heidegger's own radical appropriation of it from Schleiermacher, that he sets out to develop his **philosophical hermeneutics** which is founded on **the logic of question and answer**. This hermeneutical logic does not set out to overcome or close the historico-temporal distance between interpreter and text (i.e. the partners in a conversation) in the hope of accessing some original psychological intention, but rather to acknowledge the inevitable claim that a text makes on its reader in bringing the reader (as a finite being) into the eventful play of ontological truth, as opposed to the mere expression of individual life. The priority assigned to being, human finitude and the event of truth is evidence of Heidegger's profound influence.

Significance   Contrasted with **meaning** (See **Hirsch, E. D.**)

Skinner, Quentin (1940–)   English historian of political philosophy author of the two-volume *The Foundations of Modern Political Thought* (1978). Like Gadamer he was influenced by the work of **Collingwood**.

Socrates (469–399 BCE)   Socrates, a soldier and stonemason, was the teacher of **Plato**. He figures in many of the dialogues of Plato although there is some dispute as to whether the words put into his mouth are in fact his own or those of his literary creator. He was allegedly executed in 399 on charges of impiety and corrupting the youth of Athens. Although Socrates defended himself against such allegations, partly trumped up by his political opponents, he willing accepted his punishment and died by drinking hemlock. His philosophy, advocated by the early Plato, amounted to a procedure of detailed lawyer-type questioning (*elenchus*) in order to establish the true nature of things. Working on the assumption that the citizens of Athens, notably its politicians, used notions they were unable to define and explain exactly, Socrates went on a mission to expose this state of affairs by holding up to ridicule those who took themselves to be wise when they were not. Socrates enquires into the nature of beauty, justice, virtue and many other concepts. Significant is the fact that Socrates never wrote anything down; his philosophy was fundamentally a process of enquiry, enacted when he took disputants to task, embarrassing them into an admission of their ignorance.

Socrates is important for Gadamer for the following reasons. He prioritizes speech over writing. Philosophy is the live exchange between different parties. Because philosophy is fundamentally spoken, the written word is secondary. Secondly, the spoken dimension to philosophy reveals its other main trait, namely that it is fundamentally dialogical. Gadamer's reading

of Socrates is at odds with the view that Socratic thought was fundamentally a device for dismissing logically suspect reasoning. Although he
provokes others into dialogue and initiates the conversation he is in no way
controlling it the **matter at issue** or the topic under discussion is the real
regulator of the conversation. When Socrates likens himself to a midwife
the metaphor is appropriate. Just as the midwife is present at the birth of a
child, so Socrates is in attendance when truth emerges from a conversation.
His role is not the heroic bringer of truth but the person responsible for
setting up the right conditions whereby truth is permitted to surface within
the collective wisdom of dialogue. What Socratic dialogue demonstrates is
not a logical procedure but a way of revealing truth as it is made manifest
in a genuine conversation. For Gadamer, Socratic dialogue or **dialectic**
prefigures **hermeneutics**.

Solidarity   Although solidarity proper is only fully thematized in the
lectures and essays after *Truth and Method*, it is in many senses already
indirectly present in the major work. Solidarity, the sense of a 'shared life',
is not mentioned in *Truth and Method* but it is never far away from
the work's principal concerns. A brief summary of *Truth and Method*'s
major themes will assist in bringing out this point. Despite the manifold
threads in *Truth and Method*, one of Gadamer's principal concerns is
to highlight the all-pervasiveness of linguisticality. Following the tradition
from Hamann to **Heidegger** (and, arguably, to some extent **Wittgenstein**)
Gadamer emphasizes the expressive rather than the designative dimension
of language. Not only does this picture of language's practical rather
than designative relationship to the world militate against the subjectivist
tradition in philosophy, it asserts the priority of the communal and the
social. Language is made possible through a large measure of shared life;
we might even say that a basic solidarity is a precondition of language.
Far from passively representing the world, language constitutes it. This is
achieved through a network of communal and consensual agreements
rather than by way of a process of depiction and representation of the
already given.

The agreements sustaining language are themselves unstable, being
constantly modified in use. Language is essentially dialogical; meanings are
constantly transformed in the process of linguistic interaction and exchange.
This is best expressed in Gadamer's term the **fusion of horizons**. Language

always speaks from within a site or horizon, but that horizon is defined and limited by its relation to other horizons from which new meanings are produced. The idea of the ***fusion* of horizons** brings out quite well certain features of language and the social. As horizons are necessarily in relation to others they are constantly in the process of re-negotiation. The idea of fusion suggests the possibility of conciliation and compromise, suggesting a deep fallibility in our encounters with the other. At the same time it suggests the possibility of broadening and expanding horizons. It is at this point that we can regard fusion as an expansion not merely of experience and under-standing but as an extension of solidarities.

So for Gadamer meaning is possible and understanding and language are actualized because certain solidarities are at the heart of all our interpretative, hermeneutical enterprises. The **fusion of horizons** depends upon what Gadamer (borrowing from **R. G. Collingwood**) calls '**the logic of question and answer**'. Through this informal logic (or dialogic) of language, ever-expanding solidarities emerge. Crucially this process applies across as well as down cultures. Gadamer says little on this point but one assumes hermeneutical dialogue makes trans-cultural exchange and understanding possible: the fusion of horizons is seemingly blind to national and temporal boundaries. Since the herme-neutic process involves universality, all understanding, whatever the cultural background, participates in the **hermeneutic circle** of incompleteness, of part and whole.

Gadamer quite clearly sees the relationship between 'solidarity' and 'difference' as tension-ridden but not mutually exclusive; after all, the **fusion of horizons** arises out of **dialogue**. What Gadamer questions is radical alterity where the other is completely other. Gadamer counters radical alterity by returning to solidarity. In his 'Reply to Jacques Derrida' (Michelfelder, 1989) he accepts the limitations placed upon understanding. He cedes the possibility that meanings are dispersed and deferred when he says: 'Of course we encounter limits again and again: we speak past each other and are even at cross-purposes with ourselves'. However, the opacity and potential breakdown of meaning only occurs where some measure of agreement already exists. Failure to communicate would not be possible, Gadamer says, if 'we had not travelled a long way together ... All human solidarity, all social stability, presupposes this'. Such a comment would also apply to the **hermeneutics of suspicion** and the view that language inevitably falls victim to the hidden snares of ideology. Despite linguistic distortions through the intervening structures of power or class or gender or the vagaries of the unconscious, for the most part we need to accept that we have 'travelled a long way together' before we emphasize the degree to which we might travel apart.

Against the deconstructive thought that all dialogue is motivated by logocentrism or will to power, in a conversation with Riccardo Dottori, Gadamer offers the example of consolation: 'If I console someone who is in despair, then I am naturally seeking to make a 'we' possible – that is, I am seeking to make possible that situation of mutual understanding and solidarity that is a dialogue ... This willing to console is not will to power' (Gadamer, 2004, p. 60).

But emphasis upon solidarity in itself does not meet the criticism that Gadamer's **tradition** is so homogeneous and undialectical it appears to be a benevolent 'club of the like-minded'. Against this criticism one may offer the following two thoughts. Firstly, as Part One of *Truth and Method* so clearly illustrates, a central feature of a **dialogue** with an artwork is '**play**'. Gadamer extends the idea of play and playfulness to dialogue. Hence solidarity is not based upon static and unitary agreement but the ceaseless to-and-fro of hermeneutical play. So Gadamer's history and tradition are not static and toothless repositories of the past but larger versions of the interactive, dynamic oppositional process at work in all dialogical understanding revealed in his notion of **effective historical consciousness**. We may even speak not of the play of difference but the play of solidarity. Social life is underscored by varieties of linguistic agreement but they are in a constant free play of interpretation. Secondly, the dialectical and the hermeneutic are not that far apart; they both assume instability and a dynamic for change. Gadamer even speaks of himself as the Hegel of the 'bad infinity', not of a move to the Absolute but of an irresolvable **dialectic**.

In writings and conversations after ***Truth and Method*** Gadamer more explicitly thematizes solidarity, linking it directly to cultural and political concerns. In the essay 'The limitations of the expert' (Misgeld and Nicholson, 1993), he sees in modern cultural life an over-emphasis on the cult of specialization. This deference to the specialist is only feasible when the commonalities outlined above are overridden:

> I am convinced that even in a highly bureaucratized, thoroughly
> organized and thoroughly specialized society, it is possible to
> strengthen existing solidarities. Our public life appears to me
> to be defective in so far as there is too much emphasis on the
> different and disputed, on that which is contested or in doubt.
> What we truly have in common and what unites us thus re-
> mains, so to speak, without a voice. Probably we are harvest-
> ing the fruits of a long training in the perception of differences
> and in the sensibility demanded by it. Our historical education
> aims in this direction, our political habits permit confrontations
> and the bellicose attitude to become commonplace. In my
> view we could only gain by contemplating the deep solidarities
> underlying all norms of human life. (Misgeld and Nicholson,
> 1993 p. 192.)

The suggestion here is that the differences in status, control and power in bureaucratized societies are made manifest through specialization. Specialization can be challenged in various ways. What is common for Gadamer is not a common humanity but the brute fact that specialist knowledge, the kind that inevitably gives rise to hierarchies and uneven social power, lacks genuine authority and is essentially usurped. Returning to the dialogical nature of language and knowledge, we need to remind ourselves that the kind of control of language and the world instrumental reason seeks is unrealizable. Gadamer's picture of language is one of a ceaseless dialogue, one that is under no individual or interest group's control. His view of dialogue as fallible and corrigible militates against this. In keeping with the inheritance from German idealism, via **Nietzsche** and **Heidegger** (and again to some extent we need to include **Wittgenstein** here), Gadamer rejects the scientific-technical world-view and reacts against the idea that scientific-technological specialism overshadows underlying solidarities.

Speculative structure of language Philosophical hermeneutics reveals an important dimension to the general nature of language not usually acknowledged in the philosophy of language. Against the view that language is made up of fixed and determinate propositions, Gadamer introduces the idea that it is quite the opposite; **language** is made up of shifting and indeterminate elements and hence is at heart speculative. To say something is the case is not merely to advance an assertion, it is to place it a within a broad context or horizon of meanings. For this reason a set of minutes for a meeting will be a poor, because inadequate, description of what actually happened. It will fail to capture the said within the context of the unsaid; the unsaid in some way gives meaning to the chain of meanings in the said. Gadamer is not simply making the obvious claim that meanings are determined by context; he is asserting that the interplay between the said and the unsaid is what drives language on in to ever new semantic possibilities. Needless to say the speculative structure of language passes unnoticed in everyday linguistic exchanges; it is only with the poetic uses of language that the speculative is most evident. What Gadamer has in mind here is not transparently clear but his line of thought seems to be as follows. The use of everyday language in lyric poetry, and the power such language acquires in the juxtaposition of the said and the unsaid, opens up entirely new linguistic possibilities. Despite the fact that the language here is commonplace, it is used in new ways, and discloses aspects of being hitherto obscured. Following **Hegel**, Gadamer speaks of the speculative in the original sense of the *speculum*, a mirror, as it is the power of language, especially the language of poetry, to present and disclose (rather than reflect or represent). The idea of the speculative allows us to grasp Gadamer's central claim about language, that language has the power constantly to overreach itself and generate new meanings, and nowhere is this more apparent than in the language of poetry. (See **the poetic word**.)

Spirit (*Geist*)   (See **Hegel**.)

Speech and the spoken word   (See **linguisticality**.) As far back as the Greeks, and lasting well into the modern age, is the view that speech, the spoken word, takes logical and chronological precedence over the written word. Plato certainly advances this position with the thought that if the written word is misinterpreted there is no one to rescue it from misunderstanding. This position is dominant in the modern period, from Jean-Jacques Rousseau, who seeks to show how writing is historically antecedent to gestures and speech. In structuralist linguistics spoken symbols come before the written version. With the spoken word misunderstandings can be discussed and rectified. Gadamer subscribes to this traditional view about the superiority of speech; in fact the speech-writing relationship is at the heart of his work. Hermeneutics is described as bringing the written word out of its alienated form and returning it to its more fundamental condition, speech. The transformation of written signs back into the form of speech is the essential **dialogue** without which language would be meaningless. The real point here is that language is to be understood not as an inert repository of signs but as something that is only meaningful when it is part of a dialogical exchange, and this need not be the spoken **dialogue** of conversation. More often than not it is the dialogical interaction between text and interpreter. To bring the written word out of its enforced alienation is not just to appreciate the sense in which language is only meaningful when it is part of a socially-constructed dialogue. It is to restore the written language of a text to the world and context from which the language itself has been removed; this will have the effect of bringing to the fore neglected and forgotten meanings which are an obstruction to richer forms of understanding.

Subject-object division A central problem in western philosophy is the relationship between the knowing subject and the known object. There seems to be an unbridgeable division between an individual subject claiming to know something and the object of their knowledge because they are not intimately linked, giving rise to scepticism. Much of the history of philosophy is a series of ideas and arguments about overcoming this division. **Philosophical hermeneutics** avoids this division in the **fusion of horizons**. (See **Hegel**.)

Subjectivity To speak of a conception of subjectivity in Gadamer's thought, it is first necessary to mention the way he proposes to read the history of this concept. In his short essay 'Subjectivity and Intersubjectivity. Subject and Person', Gadamer takes up the history of the concept of subjectivity, which already appears in many earlier works, including *Truth and Method*, and it is a concept that Gadamer considers crucial and closely related to his own **philosophical hermeneutics**. His references extend throughout the entire history of Western thought in the text. In order to get closer to the meaning of subjectivity, Gadamer starts with the origin of the term 'subject'. *Hypokeimenon* is the Greek word corresponding to the subject, substrate or *subjectum*, although it in no way implies what we understand by reflective subjectivity or wilful egoity. Gadamer is at pains to point out that the Greek term *hypokeimenon* means that which stands under us or that which is thrown beneath us, and its meaning, for Aristotle at least, articulates the unchanging substratum that underlies every change or alteration, the relationship between the thing and its accidents, the substance and the matter.

The influence of **Heidegger's** critique of traditional notions of subjectivity is clearly visible in Gadamer's hermeneutics, and the concept of transcendental subjectivity is also one of the most controversial issues in the former's critique of **Husserl**. As such, Gadamer appropriates Heidegger's critique and asks what remains after critical subjectivity. Who or what comes after the subject and should we simply drop the subject altogether? However, taking a critical distance from Heidegger's notion of *Dasein*, he writes,

> 'The way Heidegger had developed the preparation of the question of Being, and the way he had worked out the understanding of the most authentic existential structure of *Dasein*, the Other could only show itself in its own existence as a limiting factor.... Heidegger's answer seemed to me to give short shrift to the phenomenon I was concerned with. It is not only that everyone is in principle limited. What I was concerned with was why I experience my own limitation through the encounter with the Other, and why I must always learn to experience anew if I am ever to be in a position to surpass my limits' (*Subjectivity and Intersubjectivity*, p. 284).

For Gadamer the terms subjectivity and intersubjectivity display conceptual weaknesses. The problem is that **Husserl** claims to be able to derive the constitution of the world from the meaning of transcendental intersubjectivity and only through co-participation in the world can we think the coexistence and the mediation of monads together. Hence we have a world only on the basis of a constituting consciousness. Yet for Gadamer the understanding of the self and the other has its own meaning beyond the language of consciousness and act-intentionality, and this is based on dialogical interpretation and understanding.

It is the above dialogical understanding of the human being that guides *Truth and Method* along the path of **philosophical hermeneutics**, and human subjectivity is challenged by means of a critique of aesthetic and historical consciousness, as well as the description of a non-instrumentalized conception of language as the constitutive medium which opens up the world, a medium which challenges the notion of an extra-mundane, autonomous and non-participating consciousness that experiences the objective nature of the world without belonging to the everyday world.

Gadamer's decisive way of challenging the notion of subjectivity is via the concept of **play**, in which he attempts to twist free from residual subjective implications in order to highlight the medial structure of play itself. It is from this hermeneutical and phenomenological investigation of being at play, being effortlessly in play, that Gadamer challenges the dogmatic notion of subjectivity.

Yet Gadamer has been criticized for putting forward a notion of language that merely plays itself out through the human being and as a result critics have argued that the notion of subject or agent has been lost to the effortlessness of the play. For instance, philosophers such as Manfred Frank, Philippe Forget and **Hans-Herbert Kögler** have criticized Gadamer for having dissolved the subject into the hermeneutic event and for having turned the event of understanding into a 'super-subject' bound up with the 'super-subjective' powers of history and **tradition**. These critics claim that Gadamer fails to separate out subjectivity, the absorbing event of language, and the to-and-fro of interpretative play, the back and forth of the event of play. In sum, then, the subject, for Gadamer, stands beneath the hermeneutical event, is played by the game, or is in thrall to historically situated play. It seems fair to say that Gadamer prioritizes the event of play over the notion of an autonomous player, and perhaps the important notion of an individuated or an autonomous subject is unfortunately lost to the game. As Gadamer puts it:

> 'Long before we understand ourselves through the process of self-examination, we understand ourselves in a self-evident way in the family, society and state in which we live. The focus of subjectivity is a distorting mirror. The self-awareness of the individual is only a flickering in the closed circuits of historical life' (*TM*, p. 278).

Symbol (See *The Relevance of the Beautiful*.)

— T —

'Text and Interpretation' 'Text and Interpretation' is an extended late article that came about as a result of Gadamer's 1981 debate with **Jacques Derrida**. The article stemmed from an invitation to participate in a conference held at the Sorbonne in Paris, a conference dedicated to the theme of 'Text and Interpretation'. Unfortunately, Gadamer's 1981 paper openly grappled with and responded to Derrida's notion of **deconstruction**, while Derrida's response to Gadamer's paper was a reading of **Heidegger**'s interpretation of **Nietzsche**, which failed to mention Gadamer by name. As such, the debate was a non-starter from the beginning and has been termed the' improbable debate'. However, Gadamer's original paper was expanded and extensively reworked prior to its publication in German in 1984 and remains one of Gadamer's most mature, thought-provoking and reflective pieces in which he tries to express the development and content of his **philosophical hermeneutics** and his understanding of **deconstruction**, to which he continued to devote himself. This essay treats such issues as his own philosophical debt to **Heidegger**, the influence of Heidegger on **Derrida**, the nature of **linguisticality** and the concept of an 'eminent text', especially the poetic text, in which language comes most fully into its own and displays its resonating power. It must be said, however, one of the most enigmatic and beautiful sentences in this text, a text which emphasizes commonality and communality throughout, is the following: 'The breath of solitude blows through everything written' (*TI*, p. 388).

Tradition The word tradition derives from the Latin verb *tradere*, to deliver, hence a tradition is the transmission, or carrying across, of something. In more recent times the word has come to refer to customs, practices and belief systems that are carried over, handed down from generation to generation. Despite the widespread respect for the authority of such things as church tradition in the medieval and early modern world, from a modernist perspective tradition comes to be viewed as a distortion of truth and knowledge and to be avoided and overcome on the grounds that it may have no other authority and justification than its own longevity and durability. This antagonism to tradition was in the mind of those supporters of the **Enlightenment** ideal who saw it as little more than uncritical obedience to customary beliefs, unchallenged by the strict and more exacting criterion of reason. Hence tradition, if it went unchallenged or failed the test of reason, is taken to be little more than myth, blind superstition, or ideas and practices observed and followed unreflectively and with no concern for the possibility that they may have an irrational grounding and foundation.

At issue here is an assumed opposition between reason on the one hand and tradition on the other. Although the thinkers of the enlightenment took for granted that reason always trumped tradition, with this view holding sway throughout the modern period, Gadamer seeks to show how tradition is not necessarily opposed to reason; in fact reason and tradition are not readily separated, being co-dependent. Gadamer disputes this opposition, seeking to reclaim the idea of tradition as a vital aspect of understanding and an irreducible component of our cultural lives. In part his challenge to the modernist orthodoxy about the irrelevance of tradition is historical. Prior to the modern age tradition was a legitimate source of authority and a legitimate basis of knowledge claims, especially the authority of scriptural and canonical texts that constituted the written tradition, and the enlightenment rejection of tradition needs to be seen in this light. For Gadamer tradition is not the dead weight of the unreflective past clouding or distorting the thought of the present, but is in fact what makes thought in the present possible, a condition of the possibility of thought itself. In order to make this position convincing, the onus is clearly on Gadamer to rethink or revive an account of tradition that is not just the inert force of the past pulling on the present but a more dynamic relationship. To do this Gadamer rejects a traditional subject and object account of knowledge. His starting point in describing the way human understanding operates is to discard the idea of a knowing subject, the kind of thinking subject described by the French philosopher **René Descartes**, for example. Gadamer's subject is constituted by **prejudices**. **Prejudices** are ultimately the linguistic practices that are inherited from the speaker's **tradition**. To speak of **prejudice** is to suggest we inhabit a distorting perspective on the world. In a sense this is true, but Gadamer's real point is that to inhabit a language is to take over a perspective, a world-view peculiar to the language itself. Language gives one a view of the world and that view is always partial, tendentious and embedded within a specific culture and place in history. The prejudices we inherit, like **tradition** (and the vehicle within which it travels, **language**), are not static and fixed.

This is the point at which Gadamer differentiates himself from the enlightenment idea of tradition as oppressive and restricting. There is a constant movement between the ceaseless realignment of a person's prejudices and tradition, such that tradition is both created and creating. Tradition bears upon the prejudices of the individual in the present and is then changed in the process. Tradition, for Gadamer, is a dynamic changing, creative force, constantly determining and determined. Subjects and objects are part of a wider formation and that is tradition.

A fuller description of the operation of tradition would involve a more detailed account of other key terms in Gadamer's lexicon, namely, the **hermeneutic circle**, **dialogue** and **historically effected consciousness**. In brief, in the activity of understanding one's prejudices come to the fore. One is never fully conscious of one's prejudices but they come into play in an act of understanding, and in seeking to understand, the hermeneutic circle comes in to play. Expressed another way, the act of understanding is always both circular and dialogical. One brings into **play** the **hermeneutic circle** and at the same time engages in a dialogue with the other. The importance here, for Gadamer, is that the act of understanding is invariably a dialogue within tradition, a dialogue whereby different aspects of tradition come into contact and 'fuse'. So there is no radical separation between subjects and objects, no scepticism about the subject and its relationship to the object as all are ultimately part of a wider formation, i.e. tradition. The culture of the past (**tradition**) is always affecting the present and making its mark on the future. This runs counter to the idea that our understanding of the world is only possible when the unencumbered self is divorced from tradition and regulated by pure reason. On the contrary, for Gadamer, the possibility of understanding presupposes an active engagement with tradition.

Gadamer's revival of the importance of tradition has been subjected to a good deal of criticism from Marxists, who suspect tradition to be fabricated in the interests of the dominant class, and from feminists who identify tradition with patriarchy.

'Transformation into structure'   Gadamer's term to suggest that art transforms the everyday world not into an aesthetic dream world but another perspective on reality:

Transformation into structure is not simply transposition into
another world. Certainly the play takes place in another,
closed world. But inasmuch as it is a structure, it is, so to
speak, its own measure and measures itself by nothing outside
it. Thus the action of a drama – in this respect it still entirely
resembles the religious act – exists as something that rests
absolutely within itself. It no longer permits of any comparison with reality as the secret measure of all verisimilitude. It
is raised above all such comparisons – and hence also above
the question of whether it is all real – because a superior truth
speaks from it (*TM*, p. 112).

The transformation [into structure] is a transformation into
the true. It is not enchantment in the sense of a bewitchment
that waits for the redeeming world that will transform things
back to what they were; rather, it is itself redemption and
transformation back into true being. In being presented in
play, what is emerges. It produces and brings into light
what is otherwise constantly hidden and withdrawn
(*TM*, p. 112).

Troeltsch, Ernst. (1865–1923)   German philosopher, theologian and
historian who studied the relationship between religion and historicism.
Influenced by Max Weber and the Baden School of Neo-Kantianism, not to
mention the latter's brand of historico-cultural value philosophy, Troeltsch
was interested in the relationship that obtains between values and history
and was inspired by both Romanticism and German Idealism. Troeltsch
constantly attempted to overcome historicism and its perceived **relativism**
by means of transcendent norms, and yet remained sensitive to the concrete
particularity of historical facts. His encounters with Weber's thought
brought to light the need to examine the relationship between Christianity
and the modern world, insofar as this relationship determines the conditions of cultural phenomena against the background of socio-economic
interests. In his late work, Troeltsch attempted to consider the ground of
values not in terms of abstract systems of thought, but rather via a material
logic of history (the material presence provided by history) that, focusing
on the relation between philosophical reflection and empirical research,

analyses life in its concreteness, seeing individual phenomena as pregnant with meaning.

Truth   (See *Truth and Method*.)

Truth and Method (1960)   The publication of this book was a defining moment in the career of Gadamer. Prior to this time his name was virtually unknown outside his native Germany and even there he was regarded as little more than a classical philologist specializing in ancient philosophy. The basic outline of *Truth and Method* as a theoretical work on hermeneutics was conceived in the early 1950s. *Truth and Method* became a seminal work of twentieth-century philosophy and Gadamer's reputation as a major thinker spread beyond continental Europe, achieving notoriety in the English-speaking world, especially in North America. *Truth and Method* first attracted the attention of those working in social theory and literary theory; only later did it achieve status as a key text in the tradition of continental philosophy.

  Gadamer's preoccupation with language is partly responsible for the 'linguistic turn' in continental thought, one that mirrored a similar turn in the philosophy of the English-speaking world of the same period. The scope of the work is vast and its erudition extensive. It incorporates a variety of ideas and motifs taken from the entire history of western philosophy. Some sense of the main themes is captured in the title and subtitle of the work: *Truth and Method: Elements of a Philosophical Hermeneutics*. For ease of exposition let us first consider the main title, *Truth and Method*. As many critics have commented the title could just as readily, perhaps more appropriately even, have had the title *Truth or Method*. The change of conjunction from 'and' to 'or' emphasizes the sense of an opposition between 'truth' and 'method' and this tension is at the heart of Gadamer's work. Although he never explicitly thematizes the concept of **truth**, it is a central concern of the work and Gadamer engages in a survey of modern philosophical thought to show that its concern with the elaboration of a precise **method**, far from disclosing truth, actually overshadows it. Methodological concerns, far from giving access to indisputable truths, distort existing culturally transmitted certainties silently carried within **tradition**. Against the claims in the modern age that **method** is the most reliable matrix and source of authority for truth, Gadamer seeks to reclaim the earlier, essentially pre-modern, dependence upon **tradition** as the legitimate source of authority that somehow gets forgotten or distorted in the modern age.

Authority is a central concern in **Truth and Method**. Gadamer argues against the idea that the sole source of authority for knowledge is a scientifically or rationally inspired **method**. He seeks to show that genuine authority and the real source of truth in human affairs are not regulated by an illusory universal reason but by what is handed down in **tradition**. This idea was taken for granted in 'literary' (that is, pre-scientific) cultures but loses currency in the modern age where the authority of **tradition** is placed in question and overshadowed by the authority of scientific method. For Gadamer, there are three central sources of traditional ('traditionary') truths and these are art, history and language, and **Truth and Method** is divided into three sections dealing at great length with these areas of concern. Part 1 is entitled 'The question of truth as it emerges in the experience of art', Part 2 'The extension of the question of truth to understanding in the human sciences' and Part 3 is entitled 'The ontological shift of hermeneutics guided by language'.

In Part1 Gadamer connects truth to art. Art theory, in the early modern period, under the influence of **Immanuel Kant**, connected art to feeling and valued art purely in terms of the emotional (the 'aesthetic') response a painting or a poem evoked in the observer or audience. This subjectivization of art Gadamer calls into question. Art, he maintains, is not principally to do with feelings and audience responses, because such a view ignores the being of the artwork itself and the truth it reveals. The truth of the artwork is not just in the artwork and not just in the response to it but in the play between the two.

In Part 2 Gadamer changes the focus away from art to the way cultures conceive of their past. This is not merely a question of the way cultures write their own histories but has more to do with how they situate themselves in relation to their own collective past. Gadamer's concern here is with the way the past and the present are interconnected and how the past is an element in the way truth is conceived: this is an idea foreign to modernism where past and present are radically separated. Gadamer's argument in this section is a detailed examination of the fortunes of the human sciences and their varying conceptions of **historicality**. The argument here is richly detailed and traces the fate of the school of **hermeneutics**. This middle section of *Truth and Method* contains the kernel of Gadamer's principal argument, that a more authentic account of truth reveals it to be not the acquisition of knowledge but a deeper understanding of what it is to be human, what it is to be an integral part of a cultural tradition that is not fixed, but dynamically changing as the past collides with the present. This understanding is fundamentally an awareness of the historical nature of our being.

Once again Gadamer takes issue with modernist or **Enlightenment** thought that effectively spirits away our **historicality** in its commitment to the idea of a universal reason. In turning to **hermeneutics**, especially the ontological version of the **hermeneutic circle**, advanced by his teacher, **Martin Heidegger**, Gadamer offers a novel account of human understanding. The hermeneutic circle of part and whole, completeness and incompleteness, is not only a picture of the structure of textual understanding; it is, further, a feature of our essentially practical relationship to the world. The circle of understanding has the following features. It is bound up with **prejudice**. This is not bigotry but the unique cultural perspective on the world through its language and tradition. Human understanding is a constant but incompletable **dialogue** with **tradition**. To establish this position Gadamer turns to disparate places within the history of western philosophy, principally **Plato** and **Aristotle**, and the English philosopher and historian **R. G. Collingwood**. Here many of the ideas and motifs in *Truth and Method* come together. Human understanding is no more than a **tradition** in constant **dialogue** with itself. In a genuine **dialogue**, the model for which is the Platonic dialogues, the participants are taken over by a fundamental concern, and there is a sense in which the fundamental concern is larger than the individual participants in the **dialogue**, just as in **play** the players are subordinate to the game. In genuine dialogue participants reach out to find mutual understanding in what Gadamer terms the **fusion of horizons**. The idea here is that although horizons may differ, they can be fused so that genuine dialogue can always take place in some form or another.

The other significant piece of terminology Gadamer coins in this section of *Truth and Method* is **effective historical consciousness**. The idea here is that consciousness is largely an effect of language and tradition through which we speak. A problem in Gadamer's claim is the role of subjectivity and individual consciousness. He seems to reduce the individual to little more than an effect of history rather than an agent. This is brought out in this passage from **Truth and Method**:

> The focus of subjectivity is a distorting mirror. The self-aware-
> ness of the individual is only a flickering in the closed circuits
> of historical life. That is why the prejudices of the individual ...
> constitute the historical reality of his being (**TM**, p. 278).

The final section of **Truth and Method** on the nature of language is perhaps the most difficult because the least polished and the most sketchy. Despite the plurality of themes in this section, the work as a whole leads up to what is one of the book's central claims and it is this: 'Being that can be understood is language' (**TM**, p. 475). The thought here is that ultimately whatever is available to human understanding is available in linguistic form. The implications of this view are many and various. It means that all understanding, whether it is through experience or reflection, is ultimately understandable because it is expressed in linguistic form. A further implication is that there is nothing understandable beyond the limits of language. A similar thought is expressed by **Ludwig Wittgenstein** in the concluding line of the *Tractatus*: 'whereof we cannot speak thereof we must stay silent'.

The motif of language (linguisticality) and its inescapability ties in with another major theme of **Truth and Method**, that of universality. Because all understanding is linguistic and because it is also hermeneutical, it also has a universal quality. What Gadamer means here is that his **philosophical hermeneutics** is universal in a double sense. It is universal because of the universality of language, that is, as noted above, because there is nothing outside language. It is universal in another sense: **hermeneutics** is a universal mode of enquiry. **Hermeneutics**, for Gadamer, is not a method or procedure for reading and understanding texts, as it was for the early hermeneuticists, but is ultimately something much broader. The **herme-neutical circle** operates, via language, in all areas of human activity and enquiry.

Gadamer's enquiry in **Truth and Method** started with an investi-gation into the nature of the human sciences and concludes that all human understanding is hermeneutical and hence universal. In fact there is a sense in which **philosophical hermeneutics** dissolves traditional philosophical enquiry into hermeneutics. This conclusion to **Truth and Method** seems quite inconsistent with its initial assumption, namely that understanding was intrinsically historical and embedded within tradition and cultural practice, and hence anything but universal. But the inconsistency is more apparent than real. For Gadamer, **universality** refers to the perspective on the universe opened up by the language through which this is given expression. So in fact there is no inconsistency but a reaffirmation of the idea that we are inscribed within a linguistic tradition.

—U—

Understanding and Interpretation In *Truth and Method*, Gadamer states that his intention is philosophical and not methodological, which means **philosophical hermeneutics** does not propose a simple methodology of understanding and interpretation. Indeed, the very title of Gadamer's magnum opus leaves us in little doubt that the author is strongly against importing the excessively rational methods of modern science into hermeneutics, arguing for a notion of a hermeneutical understanding and interpretation which are essentially irreducible to the methods of the natural sciences.

In a sense, Gadamer's goal, like **Kant**'s before him, is to inquire into the transcendental structures (i.e. the ways of being) of understanding and interpretation. In much the same way that Kant was driven by a concern to determine the condition of possibility of all knowledge and science, and not by a desire to establish a method of scientific research, so too Gadamer does not propose a methodology for the human sciences, nor does he revive the old opposition between the human sciences and the natural sciences, but moves the discussion forward, focusing instead on the forms and conditions of understanding and interpretation. Furthermore, Gadamer's work shows how hermeneutics is ontologically significant, i.e. it not only refers to the epistemological progress of certain sciences or disciplines, but also concerns the essence of human existence, the being of understanding that is operative in and through human life.

The influence of **Heidegger** on Gadamer's thought is most present here insofar as the former's existential analytic in *Being and Time* shows how understanding is not one possibility among others, a possibility that just happens to occur in the human being, but rather the unique and fundamental way of being of human existence. Hence the model of textual understanding and interpretation is, for Gadamer, the paradigm for our experience of the world in general. In this sense, ontological hermeneutics is a universal philosophical hermeneutics. However, ***Truth and Method*** aims to illustrate how the very act or event of understanding and interpretation gives voice to an experience of truth that is different from the objectively driven methodology and rationality of modern science from Galileo onwards. For Gadamer, there are specific regions of truth that do not fall under the domain of scientific methodology and these specific regions are not susceptible to epistemological acquisition. Moreover, a mindfulness of these regions of experience (e.g. artistic, historical and philosophical experience) is of fundamental importance to humanity and to a philosophical understanding of humanity.

For instance, art is for Gadamer a clear example of an extra-methodological experience of truth in that it provides understanding and interpretation with specific challenges. Gadamer is critical of the concept of transcendence in the aesthetic domain, that is, the modern way of understanding art as separate and independent from the rest of lived experience. He rejects the interpretation that has led to the segregation of art into a separate dimension of spirit. Above all, this approach has led to the uncoupling of art and truth: art no longer has any truth-value and, in opposition to the sciences, it refers only to the world of sensory appearance. From this point of view, one of the principal determinants of subjectivism in art and its exclusion from the truth is Kant who, in the *Critique of Judgement*, denied art any kind of theoretical or practical value: aesthetic experience is other than knowledge and practice.

In the second section of ***Truth and Method***, Gadamer passes through the **Romantic Hermeneutics** of **Schleiermacher** to the historical hermeneutics of **Dilthey**. Gadamer accuses **Dilthey** of being unwittingly captivated by the methodology of the natural sciences, as if the problem of hermeneutical experience could be addressed by an appeal to historiographical method and psychic experience that understands historical truth as a universally objective fact. In other words, Dilthey's historicism, despite having defended historicity as the object of historiography, forgot the historical being of the historical subject and its relationship to truth.

Human understanding, however, is for Gadamer always historically determined and is always given in pre-understanding. Referring to paragraph 32 of *Being and Time*, where Heidegger introduces the concept of the **hermeneutic circle**, interpretation is understood as an articulation, unfolding and development from out of understanding. As such, Heidegger came to see in the **hermeneutic circle** the ontological structure of understanding itself, which always presupposes a prior understanding of reality, one which is rooted in the convictions of everyday human beings, and always moves in a circular fashion. It is precisely for this reason that the human being cannot claim to approach the world free of assumptions and prejudices, and it is this inability to operate without prejudice which Heidegger calls our 'being-thrown'. In a word, nothing is given to understanding as immediate and it is an illusion to claim that we are confronted by the given as unmediated. Hence Heidegger's discussion of the hermeneutic circle defines this existential-ontological structure as an inescapable human determination and as an expression of the existential fore-structure of *Dasein*'s understanding, what he terms 'fore-having', 'fore-sight', and 'fore-conception'. It is therefore not a case of exiting the hermeneutic circle, which is impossible, but rather of entering it at the right place and of remaining there appropriately, i.e. ensuring that it is not the case of received common opinion or imposed preconceptions that guides our understanding, but rather an understanding which emerges from, and is at the service of, the things themselves.

For instance, the interpreter always stands before a given text with a prior understanding of it of which he/she should be mindful, and it is precisely between this prior understanding and the impact of the operative **matter at issue** in the text that understanding takes place. These strong convictions led Gadamer to reassess the concept of prejudice that the modern tradition, and especially the Enlightenment, condemned and criticized. In fact, with the **Enlightenment**, the word prejudice acquires an essentially negative meaning, even if the word itself expresses nothing more than an opinion prior to an examination of all the relevant factors yet to be judged. **Prejudice** becomes synonymous with unfounded opinion. The **Enlightenment**, however, is itself based on prejudice, namely, the prejudice against prejudice. The rejection of prejudice, which is a constituent part of modern thought, is indicative of the disregard for the finitude of the historical individual in its attempt to attain a standpoint that is independent of the observer or interpreter. The **Enlightenment** identifies two basic types of prejudice, those due to our personal predilections and those derived from authority. Gadamer is particularly interested in these latter biases and their rejection by Enlightenment thinkers, which reaches its culmination with the Kantian declaration: 'Have courage to use your own reason!' Thus authority is taken to be synonymous with prejudice, the antithesis of reason and freedom. In reality, for Gadamer authority does not necessarily mean the blind obedience of an irrational mind, but rather a form of authority that has been present since Romanticism and much in need of rehabilitation, namely tradition.

According to Gadamer, the Romantic's way of understanding the notion of tradition appears as an equal and opposite error to that of the **Enlightenment**. The Enlightenment's faith in reason, purged of all 'authority', stands in opposition to the unconditional faith in truth found in the Romantic tradition, before which reason should fall silent. For Gadamer, listening to the tradition does not imply a passive and dogmatic acceptance of the past, but rather a free, recognitional and rational act of renewing ownership of what once was and what continues to make itself felt. If understood in this way, the conservation of the past is as much a liberating act as it is subversion and renewal.

Against the backdrop and reception of Heidegger's phenomenological-hermeneutic analysis of understanding and interpretation, Gadamer develops the key concepts of his philosophical hermeneutics: temporal distance, the historically effected consciousness, an awareness of historical determination, and the **fusion of horizons**. As we have said, the condition of hermeneutic experience is pre-understanding, which structures our set of prejudices, which testifies to our being-thrown, i.e. our belonging to a historical situation, a tradition, that binds the interpreter and interpreted together in the same historical process. Regarding the problem of temporal distance, Gadamer introduces the theory of familiarity and strangeness, i.e. the theory of simultaneous proximity to and distance from interpreter and interpreted. The temporal distance between interpreter and interpreted is not, unlike historicism argued, an obstacle to get over, but rather the constitutive condition of understanding itself.

Another key issue in Gadamer's **philosophical hermeneutics** is the history of effects, which is always essential when you want to set in relief the significance of a work or a historical fact. It is worth emphasizing that Gadamer is not so much interested in the operational aspects of this concept, which leads him to recognize that the history of an author or a work also includes the history of what was said (and not said) in this work or by that author. For Gadamer, what is important is an awareness that the history of effects is always already acting on us, that when we stand before a historical event we are never in a situation of mere abstraction or disinterested position-taking, but are always already immersed in our prior, situated understanding of the event.

The history of effects and the chain of past interpretations, in which interpretative understanding is situated and to which it responds, albeit at times unconsciously, is mediated by its object. This occurs because interpreting a text or an event is made possible because the text and the interpreter originally belong to a horizon that both transcends the present historical epoch and sustains it. Thus the history of effects is the consciousness of historical determinations, a consciousness of the shaping powers of history, an awareness of its effective force or pull, if you will. By this Gadamer means that consciousness is both simultaneously exposed to the effects of history and inextricably caught up with them.

Another fundamental concept is that of **fusion of horizons**. In accordance with the dispute with historicism, which demands that the interpreter disregards his/her own horizon for the sake of the other's horizon, Gadamer argues that there are not two separate horizons, but one larger horizon against which human life originates and is handed down. Thus, historicism's radical transposition of the past is replaced with Gadamer's **fusion of horizons**, which does not do away with the irreducible individuality of the other's horizons but rather mediates respectfully between the two. Emphasizing the novelty and event of understanding rather than the clarity and supremacy of understanding better, Gadamer writes: 'Understanding is not, in fact, understanding better, either in the sense of superior knowledge of the subject because of clearer ideas or in the sense of fundamental superiority of conscious over unconscious production. It is enough to say that we understand in a *different way, if we understand at all*' (**TM**, p. 296).

Gadamer also addresses the various stages of understanding and interpretation, arguing that the ancients distinguished between understanding, explanation and application. Romanticism subsequently identified the first two steps, that of understanding and explanation, because explanation was no longer seen as an additional act to understanding, but rather as an extended form of understanding. However, this fusion of understanding and explanation caused the Romantics to forget the third step, namely application. Gadamer is convinced that every form of understanding always has applicative consequences in the present. **Application** thus involves an actualization of the past according to the expectations and needs of the present. This notion of application, brought out most fully in Gadamer's Platonically inspired analysis of the **logic of question and answer**, reveals a way of being which is intimately tied up with knowing one's way about as an essentially dialogical task that finds understanding and interpretation to be most fully present in their concrete enactment. **Philosophical hermeneutics**, as a dialogically inspired form of thought, is not an attempt to reconstruct the original intention of the author, but rather to respond to the fact that we are called into question by the text, that we as interpreters are simultaneously interrogated by the text when we put questions to the text. In the end, the questions we pose to the text, and which it in turn poses to us, seek to recover, understand and interpret the original question to which the text was a response.

Unencumbered self The 'unencumbered self' is an idea implicit in traditional liberal political theory where the individual is taken to be separable from a specific historical and cultural location. In opposition to this idea is the '**embedded self**' where selfhood is defined precisely by those characteristics of a specific historical and cultural location. In other words, the embedded self denies the possibility of the unencumbered self. The notion of the embedded self is now common currency in postmodern, political and feminist theory. Gadamer's notion of selfhood is embedded rather than unencumbered. (See **subjectivity** and the **closed circuits of historical life**.)

Universality Traditionally, **hermeneutics** was the art of interpreting texts. In the hands of Gadamer hermeneutics acquires a universal significance. Following **Heidegger**, Gadamer claims that the incomplete – and incompletable – circle of **understanding** has an ontological significance. He makes the circle of understanding the heart of all our interpretations of the world. Put simply, all understanding is hermeneutic hence hermeneutics has universal significance. Hermeneutic understanding has this universal dimension because, for Gadamer, there is nothing outside the domain of this understanding. Everything we do or experience in the world, whether it is engagement in science, or the human sciences, or art or even philosophy, is ultimately an aspect of universal hermeneutic **understanding** in that it has the circular structure of incompleteness. All understanding is hermeneutical; it is also linguistical. The claim here is that whatever one claims to understand must also be capable of being articulated; there can be no non-linguistical understanding. For this reason language itself has this universal application. On the question of the universality of hermeneutic understanding, **Jürgen Habermas** has taken issue with Gadamer (See **Gadamer-Habermas debate**).

— **V** —

Validity in Interpretation   (See **Hirsch.**)

Vattimo, Gianni, (1936–)   Gianni Vattimo is one of the leading Italian hermeneutic thinkers and is the founder of a school of philosophy known as 'weak thought' (*il pensiero debole*). Vattimo was a student of the Italian philosopher Luigi Pareyson and later a student of Hans-Georg Gadamer. Vattimo is an original interpreter of Friedrich **Nietzsche** and Martin **Heidegger**, and as such his name is inextricably bound up with contemporary **philosophical hermeneutics** of which he is one of the leading exponents. Because Vattimo's main works were not translated into English until recent years, his international reputation is connected to some of the most important contemporary thinkers, namely, **Derrida**, **Rorty**, and **Habermas**. Vattimo is one of the most important interpreters of contemporary continental thought and he is one of the main inspirations behind the weakening of truth claims with regard to the grand narratives of rational **Enlightenment** emancipation. In addition to this,

his work revolves around such themes as the ontology of the real, the unavoidable breakdown of universal values, nihilism and Christianity, the end of modernity and a meditation on the destiny of the West in the wake of **Heidegger**.

From this standpoint, Vattimo's entire philosophical path, starting from his engagement with Nietzsche and Heidegger, is at the service of developing a theory of interpretation in relation to the hermeneutical theory of his teacher, Luigi Pareyson, which looked at the problem of Christian ethics and their roots in the concept of piety. It is in Pareyson (and subsequently in Gadamer) that we find Vattimo's intellectual debt, a debt that remains evident in most of his works, even if the results are far removed from the positions of his respective masters. Vattimo comes to Pareyson first, in addition to the attention he pays to Heidegger's interest in aesthetics, religion and the philosophy of freedom. It is to aesthetics, however, that he devotes most of his early work, even if aesthetics will always be to the forefront of his thought.

A further issue that Vattimo inherits from Pareyson is the centrality of the phenomenon of religious horizon in the interpretation of the history of modern philosophy. Pareyson argues for the weakening of Hegelianism, a more moderate Hegelianism, and his work on thinkers engaged in religious debate, such as Feuerbach and Kierkegaard, allowed him to rediscover a religious impulse at the heart of modernity that Hegel's historical rationalism had largely marginalized. Consequently, Vattimo inherits a mindfulness of the religious heritage of the Christian West and he understands religious experience, in contrast to a more liberal interpretation, as a progressive evolution in Western thought and culture leading to a Christian principle of secularism, i.e. a movement that began with Christ himself who challenged the oppressive and judgmental God of the Old Testament. Thus according to Vattimo, the secularization of the modern world which has largely replaced religious beliefs is not the result of our forsaking the source of good, but is instead the result of a process that had its beginning in Jesus Christ himself, who expressed and embodied God's love for His creation. Hence it is only in one's finite, free and situated interpretation of God's commandment 'to love', and not in church doctrine, that Vattimo believes one can achieve salvation.

Vattimo follows a similar path to Heidegger and interprets the history of Being from the perspective of its completion: the forgetting of ontological difference and the history of being in the technical world of industrial society reveals that the entire history of Western thought is pervaded by the desire to reduce the horizon of being to the domain of man's determining comprehension of being. Thus Vattimo interprets the history of Being as displaying the gradual abandonment of the origins of Greek thought (from the metaphysical identification of being with nature in Parmenides, or real being and the highest value in Plato) and the forgetting of the positively negative event that silently embodies the fate of metaphysics and the essence of Western thought. The history of Western thought, then, from Greece to the present, is interpreted as a long process of departing from the origins of a dominant metaphysical thinking and moving towards a principle of non-subjectivistic freedom in which being as pure presence gives way to the multiplicity of events. For Vattimo, this opens up the way for an historical ontology of genuine freedom, that is nonetheless far from having the last word on the matter. If Pareyson's ontology interpreted freedom as superior and more original than being, then for Vattimo the two terms become synonymous. As such, for Vattimo the notion of hope is all about holding out hope for a largely secularized world, a movement of seculari- zation that is always on the way to an as yet unfulfilled secularization.

Vattimo's 're-spiritualization' of hermeneutic experience and his analysis of reality in the postmodern situation arise in particular from the conse- quences of our recent mass communication society, where the amount of information and the interpretation of various events are multiplying exponentially, all of which gives us the impression that the facts themselves have lost their power. This is linked to the increasing importance that the notion of 'event' plays in our society through the mass media, which multi- plies the singularity and particularity of each and every event to infinity, relegating the singularity of these events to the margins of the limitless. The philosophy that acknowledges and is concerned with the centrality of **interpretation** is **hermeneutics**, a position that Vattimo formulates and expounds in his book *Truth and Interpretation*, which appeared a few years after its systematization by Gadamer.

Vattimo's interest in Gadamer's philosophical hermeneutics stems from its recognition of the primacy of interpretation within post-Hegelian philosophy and its movement towards the multifaceted nature of truth, which no longer remains confined to a single act of perception, to act intentionality, to epistemic accomplishment or to assertoric propositions, but which is the result a complex process of historically situated and dialogically mediated interpretations. **Hermeneutics**, for Vattimo, along with its theory of interpretation and its ontology of language, is the building blocks of thought, which can also be defined as a nihilistic hermeneutic ontology, i.e. a contemporary interpretation that affirms Gadamer's well known saying that 'being which can be understood is language', but which also supplements it with a fidelity to the Heideggerian demand for a non-metaphysical understanding of nihilism and the forgetting of Being. In more recent times, Vattimo's reflections have been oriented in two directions: first, he stresses that religious questions have led him to confront some of the more obscure and less easily secularized human experiences, such as evil and suffering, posing difficult questions for a philosophy that claims to address an ontology of actuality. Secondly, Vattimo has started to inquire into the character of the political, not content merely to observe the events of our time, but also to become aware that political praxis, since antiquity, has been the sole movement of emancipation and the definition of man's very essence.

Von Ranke, Leopold. (1795–1886) German historian who engaged in a tireless methodological effort to shed light on the inaccuracies and shortfalls of previous historiography. Ranke produced a series of works that emerged from meticulous research at various archives in Germany and Italy. Ranke, the founder of the school of historical method, searches for the grounds of historical objectivity and his ideal is a philological panopticon of knowledge. Ranke sees the completion of historical knowledge in the ideal of *omnia simul*, that is, in a divine vision of time. For Ranke, every event must be understood within the totality of universal world history, which has no *telos* outside itself. Inspired by Hegel, Ranke argued that there is a profound need to understand that the human being is a genuine historical happening, a singular manifestation of the eternal, and all history is subject to this eternal manifestation. Although existing in time, the historian should, according to Ranke, come as close as possible to this panoramic and impartial view of time and history, which could only be had in its purity from a transcendent perspective. Hence seeing history as part of divine knowledge or divine vision ultimately means denying the possibility that mankind can know history, and its place within the singular happening of history, in its fullness, insofar as it would require the knowledge of all the endless historical connections that bind history together in its entirety.

—W—

'Who am I and who are you?'   In his essay 'Who am I and Who are you?' a reading of the poetic cycle, 'Breath turn' (*Atemwende*) or 'Breathcrystal' (*Atemkristall*) by the poet **Paul Celan**, Gadamer analyses the ways the reader's sense of individuation and identity is disoriented and unsettled in the engagement with these verses. He says, 'we do not know at the outset, on the basis of any distanced overview or preview, what *I* or *You* means here (in Celan's poems) or whether I is the I of the poet referring to himself, or the I that is each of us. This is what we must learn.' (Gadamer, 1997, p. 70). The whole question of who is addressing whom in the decontextualised zone of the poetic, where language is effectively unhinged from its customary sites, raises important questions for **philosophical hermeneutics**. With the usual semantic reference points distorted and dislocated in the poem, the hermeneutical task is more demanding, as Gadamer admits. Words extend themselves, moving into new and hitherto unknown spaces in the **tradition**. (See **Paul Celan**.)

Wittgenstein, Ludwig (1889–1950)   Ludwig Wittgenstein was one of the most important philosophers of the twentieth century. He was born in Vienna to a wealthy family and was trained as an engineer. He moved to England to study aeronautics and developed an interest in philosophy. He studied philosophy in Cambridge with Bertrand Russell and after the First World War, when he fought for the Austrian army, he published his *Tractatus Logico-Philosophicus* (1922), a dense and cryptic treatise on the relationship between language and the world. Convinced that this work had effectively solved all the major philosophical problems, he subsequently trained as a schoolteacher, helped his sister in the design of her house in Vienna, and then worked in a monastery garden. By the late 1920s he began to see problems with his earlier philosophical work and was drawn back to the academic life. From 1929 until the end of his life he taught philosophy in Cambridge where he achieved the status of professor. His later work, after 1929, was a complete repudiation of his earlier *Tractatus*. He developed a completely novel and radical account of the nature of language which was expressed in his posthumously published *Philosophical Investigations* (1953), one of the seminal texts on the nature of language and language's relationship to the world and philosophy.

The central idea in the *Investigations* is the notion of a 'language-game'. What is a language-game? Although this is a key term in Wittgenstein's later work it is an elusive one and covers many possibilities. Wittgenstein steadfastly resists hard and fast definitions: the language-game militates against such Socratic closure. One of the reasons for likening language to a game is to highlight its imprecision and failure to divide into neatly circumscribed concepts. There can be no set of necessary and sufficient conditions to which language must conform. Instead he points to a loosely textured, open-ended picture of language: an antidote to his own Tractarian, rigid schematization of a unitary and strictly logical language. The very elusiveness of the language-game idea is illustrated by the constant changes in the way the term is written. What is the difference between 'language game' and 'language-game'? And what is the difference between '*language*-game' and '*language-game*' and the many other possible permutations scattered throughout the *Investigations*?

Wittgenstein likens everyday language to a series of overlapping and inter-related games or 'language-games' in order to counteract and expose certain well-established but fundamentally misguided conceptions of how language acquires meaning and how that meaning is sustained and disseminated. The comparison between language and game effectively undermines 'mentalist' accounts of meaning where the word achieves its effect through a direct connection to the inner workings of subjective consciousness. The totality of the game, that is the rules and social practices surrounding them, supplants the monadic isolation of the thinking 'I'.

Gadamer's dialogical account of language is very close to Wittgenstein. In fact although Gadamer does not speak of 'language-games' he does, as we have already noted in relation to aesthetics, bring out the playful element within language. And the **play** is not just to illustrate the sense in which meanings are constantly in the process of creation and recreation; it shows how meanings are beyond the control of the individual linguistic players. Once gain we see a similarity with Wittgenstein. The 'language-game' is devised to show how language is essentially practical – just as there is no game without people to play it, there can be no language without people to speak it and use it. In the case of both Gadamer and Wittgenstein there can be no real making sense of language from a theoretical perspective, no philosophy of language; language is essentially a practical activity, and can never be made an object of quasi-scientific investigation. For both Gadamer and Wittgenstein everyday language is in order as it is. The suggestion from some philosophers that language needs to be reformed and radically overhauled or turned into a more technical and precise means of communication is far from the thoughts of Gadamer and the later Wittgenstein. Both thinkers are aware of the possible traps language might set for the unwary; becoming ensnared in dangerous metaphysics is something to which they are both alert.

When philosophers use a word – 'knowledge', 'being', 'object', 'I', 'proposition', 'name' – and try to grasp the essence of the thing, one must always ask oneself: is the word ever actually used in this way in the language which is its original home? What we do is to bring words back from their metaphysical to their everyday use. Despite the dangerous temptation to use language in the service of metaphysics, Wittgenstein reminds us that language is first and foremost the language of the everyday, untainted by metaphysical aberrations. Gadamer echoes this sentiment when he distances himself from Heidegger. **Heidegger** spoke of the 'language of metaphysics' and how it had found its way into all forms of speech. Against this Gadamer offers the following Wittgensteinian thought:

> 'Is it the language of metaphysics alone that achieves this
> continual coming-to-language of our Being-in-the-world? Cer-
> tainly it is the language of metaphysics, but further behind it is
> the language of the Indo-Germanic peoples that makes such
> thinking capable of being formulated. But can a language – or
> a family of languages – ever properly be called the language of
> metaphysical thinking, just because metaphysics was thought,
> or what would be more, anticipated in it? Is not language
> always the language of the homeland and the process of
> becoming-at-home in the world?' (Heidegger's Ways 78)

In other ways also the similarities are remarkable. Both adopt a deep suspicion of scientism and the need to see all achievements in terms of scientific respectability, and they share a common suspicion of technology and the general capacity of modernity to overshadow deeper truths. But Wittgenstein is not Gadamer. There are differences in style and substance. First, let us deal with the matter of style. Increasingly in Wittgenstein's later work his style is fragmentary and aphoristic. This is in part to do with his way of working, that is, the short descriptive account of the ways a certain word, concept or phrase is used in everyday language. It also has to do with his desire to highlight the particularity of things, the need to keep away from that malignant philosophical urge he terms a 'craving for generality'. Gadamer on the other hand is more traditional and less experimental in his writing. At the same time we might say his style reflects his thought; for Gadamer the stress is not upon the unique and the particular but what it is that we as language-users actually share and have in common. For Gadamer, there is in the modern age too much stress upon difference and not enough attention to what in fact binds us as a species, what we have in common.

Word, (See **linguisticality**.)

World Displaying a fidelity to both **Husserl** and **Heidegger**, the concept of world as horizon is a central leitmotif in Gadamer's thought. Yet the **horizon of all horizons**, to use Husserl's term, is language itself as Gadamer conceives it, the world as a set of meanings which are constituted by means of discursive practices, starting from the need to express reasons and to understand the reasons of other linguistic beings. As Gadamer puts it: 'Whoever has language "has" the world' (**TM**, p. 499). Hence when Gadamer talks about understanding he is not simply referring to our ability to determine the sense of things, but our ability to experience the world as such. In other words, understanding, which is always linguistic understanding, determines our relationship with others and with the world.

For Gadamer language appears as the principle of all understanding and it underpins all social mediation, mediation that cannot be conceived in terms of the objectivity of the concept, but rather as the coming to an agreement through communication that is mutually understandable against the horizon of a shared world. Language is hence not an objective or objectifying tool but the determining dimension in which man lives. Gadamer's famous statement 'Being that can be understood is language' asserts that the world of understanding is always linguistically mediated and that every encounter is an encounter with the world that emerges in and through language. What emerges in linguistic comprehension is being itself, insofar as being belongs to self-understanding. Thus language is the coming into language of being and world. The human being will never be able to embrace the totality of language and therefore will never have full access to being or world as such. This is the case because speaking is never complete and the life of language itself is always on the way to language against the horizon of the world.

Inspired by Heidegger's *The Origin of the Work of Art*, to which he wrote the original introduction, Gadamer argues that the contemporary world experiences the work of art entirely detached from the world in which it took shape, and that the artist is increasingly deprived of his/her own historical way of being in the world, becoming nomadic and homeless in the world.

According to Gadamer, modern aesthetic experience has become 'subjectivized' and this he attributes to **Kant** who reduced art to abstract imagination, which is devoid of any dimension of truthfulness, causing art to depart from its original vocation of preparing the way for the political and moral freedom of man. On the other hand, Gadamer commends **Hegel** for having recognized the genuine nature of art and its relation to truth. However, the great shortfall of Hegel's thought consists in reducing the role of art to philosophy, i.e. proposing its overcoming in philosophy.

The work of art is not only the product of a brilliant artist; the moment of creativity never ends, but is rather conducted through the mediation of interpretation as a response to the questions which the artwork poses in opening up a new world. Thus the fluid identity of the work, its truth and its continuity are open to the future and to the world to come.

Yorck von Wartenburg, Ludwig, (1759–1830) According to Gadamer, Yorck explicates and details 'the structural correspondence between life and self-consciousness already developed in Hegel's *Phenomenology*' (***TM***, p. 243). The only way to apprehend life in its movement, Yorck argues, is to become conscious of historical life living itself and not to take a detached reflective view of life. As Gadamer puts it, showing Yorck's metaphysical continuity with Hegel, 'self-consciousness [...] folds back on and returns to itself' (*TM*, p. 244). Together with **Dilthey**, and foreshadowing **Husserl**'s phenomenology of the lifeworld, Yorck attempted to outline the historical way of being-alive proper to the human being and emphasized the lived situation of being-alive that remains hidden from dogmatic metaphysics.

BIBLIOGRAPHY

The *Gadamer Dictionary* indicates the year works were first published in their original language. This Bibliography indicates, wherever possible, the year of publication of an English translation.

i PRINCIPAL WORKS BY GADAMER

Truth and Method, trans. Weinsheimer, J. and Marshall, D. G., Second revised edition, (London: Continuum, 1975).

Philosophical Hermeneutics, edited and trans. David E. Linge, (Berkeley: University of California Press, 1976).

Hegel's Dialectic: Five Hermeneutical Studies, trans. P. Christopher Smith, (New Haven: Yale University Press, 1989).

Dialogue and Dialectic: Eight Hermeneutical Studies on Plato, (New Haven: Yale University Press, 1980).

'The Eminent Text and its Truth', *The Bulletin of the Midwest Modern Language Association*, Vol. 13, No. 1 (Spring, 1980), pp. 3–10.

Reason in the Age of Science, trans. Frederick G. Lawrence (Cambridge: The MIT Press, 1981).

Philosophical Apprenticeships, trans. Robert R. Sullivan (Cambridge: MIT Press, 1985).

The Idea of the Good in Platonic-Aristotelian Philosophy, trans. P. Christopher Smith (New Haven: Yale University Press, 1986a).

The Relevance of the Beautiful and Other Essays, edited Robert Bernasconi, and trans. Nicholas Walker (Cambridge: Cambridge University Press, 1986b).

'The History of Concepts and the Language of Philosophy', *International Studies in Philosophy*, 18, pp. 1–16, 1986c.

Plato's Dialectical Ethics: Phenomenological Interpretations Relating to the 'Philebus', trans., R. M. Wallace, (New Haven: Yale University Press, 1991).

Hans-Georg Gadamer on Education, Poetry, and History: Applied Hermeneutics, trans. Dieter Misgeld and Graeme Nicholson (Albany: State University of New York, 1992.

Heidegger's Ways, trans. John W. Stanley (Albany: State University of New York Press, 1994).

The Enigma of Health: The Art of Healing in a Scientific Age, trans. Jason Gaiger and Nicholas Walker, (Cambridge: Polity Press, 1996).

Gadamer on Celan: 'Who am I and who are you?' and other essays, eds and trans., Heinemann, R., and Bruce Krajewski, (Albany, NY: State University of New York Press, 1997).

Hermeneutics, Religion, and Ethics, trans. Joel Weinsheimer (New Haven: Yale University Press, 1999).

Literature and Philosophy in Dialogue: Essays in German Literary Theory, trans. Paslick, R. H., (Albany, NY: State University of New York Press, 1994).

'Reflections On My Philosophical Journey' (An Autobiographical Essay), in Lewis E. Hahn, (ed.), *The Philosophy of Hans-Georg Gadamer*, (Chicago: Open Court, 1997). (This is also contained in *The Gadamer Reader: A Bouquet of the Later Writings* (2007) as 'Autobiographical Reflections').

The Beginning of Philosophy, trans. Rod Coltman, (New York: Continuum, 2000).

The Gadamer Reader: A Bouquet of the Later Writings, trans. Richard E. Palmer (Evanston: Northwestern University Press, 2007).

For Gadamer bibliographies see:

Makita, Etsuro, (ed.), *Gadamer-Bibliographie (1922–1994)*, (Frankfurt am Main: P. Lang, 1995), online at http://www.ms.kuki.tus.ac.jp/KMSLab/makita/gdmhp/ghp_gabi_d.html).

Palmer, Richard, 'Bibliography of Hans-Georg Gadamer: A selected bibliography' in Lewis E. Hahn, (ed.), *The Philosophy of Hans-Georg Gadamer*, (Chicago: Open Court, 1997).

'Bibliography' in Gadamer, H-G, *Gadamer in Conversation: Reflections and Commentary*, (With Karsten Dutt et al.)., edited and trans., Palmer, Richard E., (New Haven: Yale University Press, 2001).

'Bibliography' in Dostal, Robert. J., (ed.) in *The Cambridge Companion to Gadamer*, (Cambridge: Cambridge University Press, 2002), pp. 283–312.

ii INTERVIEWS WITH GADAMER

(The best introductions to the work of Gadamer are the interviews listed below. Gadamer always considered that he was at his best when engaging in dialogue rather than when putting his thoughts on paper. Such a view is clearly consistent with his hermeneutical philosophy, which gives priority to the dialogue and conversation over the monologue that is the formal treatise or theoretical work).

Boyne, Roy, 'Interview with Hans-Georg Gadamer', in *Theory, Culture & Society*, Vol. 5, pp. 25–34. (1988).

Gadamer, Hans-G, 'Without poets there is no philosophy': Interview with Hans-Georg Gadamer', (with Christiane Gehron and Jonathan Rée), *Radical Philosophy*, 69, (Jan/Feb 1995).

Gadamer, H-G, *Gadamer in Conversation: Reflections and Commentary*, (with Karsten Dutt et al.)., edited and trans., Palmer, Richard E., (New Haven: Yale University Press, 2001).

Gadamer, H-G, *Century of Philosophy: Hans Georg Gadamer in Conversation with Riccardo Dottori*, (London: Continuum 2004).

Gadamer, H-G 'A look back over the collected works and their effective history'

(Interview with Jean Grondin) in Palmer, Richard E. ed., The *Gadamer Reader: A Bouquet of the Later Writings* (2007).

Grieder, Alfons, 'A conversation with Hans-Georg Gadamer', *Journal of the British Society for Phenomenology*, Vol. 26, No. 2, pp. 116–126. (1992).

iii SELECTED WORKS ABOUT GADAMER AND HERMENEUTICS

Bernstein, Richard J., *Beyond Objectivism and Relativism: Science, Hermeneutics and Praxis*, (Pennsylvania: University of Pennsylvania Press, 1983).

Davey, Nicholas. P., *Unquiet Understanding: Gadamer's Philosophical Hermeneutics*, (Albany: State University of New York Press, 2006).

Dostal, Robert. J., (ed.), *The Cambridge Companion to Gadamer*, (Cambridge: Cambridge University Press, 2002).

Grondin, Jean, *Introduction to Philosophical Hermeneutics*, trans. Joel Weinsheimer, (New Haven: Yale University Press, 1994).

Grondin, Jean, *Sources of Hermeneutics*, (Albany: State University of New York Press, 1995).

Grondin, Jean, *The Philosophy of Gadamer*, trans. Kathryn Plant (Chesham, Acumen, 2003).

Grondin, Jean, *Hans-Georg Gadamer: A Biography*, (New Haven: Yale University Press, 2003).

Hahn, Lewis E. (ed.), *The Philosophy of Hans-Georg Gadamer*, The Library of Living Philosophers Volume XXIV, (Chicago: Open Court, 1997).

Jasper, David, *A Short Introduction to Hermeneutics*, (London: Westminster John Knox Press, 2004).

Malpas, Jeff, Arnswald, Ulrich, Kertscher, Jens, (eds) *Gadamer's Century: Essays in Honour of H-G Gadamer*, (Cambridge: MIT Press, 2002).

Michelfelder, Diane P. & Palmer, Richard E. (eds) *Dialogue and Deconstruction: The Gadamer-Derrida Encounter*, (New York: State University of New York Press, 1989).

Lawn, Chris, *Wittgenstein and Gadamer: Towards a Post-Analytic Philosophy Of Language*, (New York and London: Continuum, 2004).

Lawn, Chris, *Gadamer: A Guide for the Perplexed*, (New York and London: Continuum, 2006).

Polt, Richard, *Heidegger: An Introduction*, London: UCL Press, 1999).

Scheibler, Ingrid, *Gadamer: Between Heidegger and Habermas*, (Lanham: Rowman & Littlefield, 2000).

Schmidt, Lawrence K., (ed.), *Language and Linguisticality in Gadamer's Hermeneutics*, (Lanham: Lexington Books, 2000).

Schmidt, Lawrence K., *The Epistemology of Hans-Georg Gadamer*, (Frankfurt: Peter Lang, 1985).

Schmidt, Lawrence, K. *Understanding Hermeneutics*, (Chesham: Acumen, 2006).

Sullivan, Robert R., *Political Hermeneutics: The Early Thinking of Hans-Georg Gadamer*, (University Park: Pennsylvania State University Press, 1989).

Wachterhauser, Brice R. (ed.), *Hermeneutics and Modern Philosophy*, (New York: SUNY Press, 1986).

Wachterhauser, Brice R. (ed.), *Hermeneutics and Truth*, (Evanston: Northwestern University Press, 1995).

Warnke Georgia, *Gadamer: Hermeneutics, Tradition and Reason*, (Cambridge: Polity Press, 1987).

Weinsheimer, Joel, *Gadamer's Hermeneutics: A Reading of 'Truth and Method'*, (New Haven: Yale University Press, 1985).

Wright, Kathleen (ed.), *Festivals of Interpretation: Essays on Hans-Georg Gadamer's Work*, (Albany: State University of New York Press, 1990).

iv OTHER RELEVANT WORKS

Gjesdal, Kristin, *Gadamer and the Legacy of German Idealism*, (Cambridge: Cambridge University Press, 2009).

Grondin, Jean, *Introduction to Philosophical Hermeneutics*, (New Haven: Yale University Press, 1991).

Hirsch, Eric D., *Validity in Interpretation*, (New Haven: Yale University Press, 1967).

Hollinger, Robert, ed. *Hermeneutics and Praxis* (Notre Dame: University of Notre Dame Press, 1985).

Hoy, David Couzens. *The Critical Circle: Literature, History, and Philosophical Hermeneutics* (Berkeley: University of California Press, 1978).

Ormiston, Gayle L. & Schrift, Alan D. (eds), *The Hermeneutic Tradition: Ast to Ricoeur*, (Albany: State University of New York Press, 1990).

Palmer, Richard E., *Hermeneutics*, (Evanston: Northwestern University Press, 1969).

Rorty, Richard, *Philosophy and the Mirror of Nature*, (Princeton: Princeton University Press, 1979).

Rorty, Richard, 'Being that can be understood is language: Rorty on Gadamer', *London Review of Books*, Vol. 22, No. 6, March 16 2000, pp. 23–25.

Schmidt, Lawrence K. (ed.), *The Specter of Relativism: Truth, Dialogue and Phronesis in Philosophical Hermeneutics*, (Evanston: Northwestern University Press, 1995).

Silverman, Hugh J. (ed.), *Gadamer and Hermeneutics*, (London: Routledge, 1991).